FEAR

THICH NHAT HANH

FEAR

ESSENTIAL WISDOM FOR GETTING THROUGH THE STORM

HarperOne
An Imprint of HarperCollinsPublishers

HarperOne

HarperCollins website: http://www.harpercollins.com

HarperCollins®, ☕®, and HarperOne™ are trademarks of HarperCollins Publishers.

ISBN 978–0–06–200472–7

CONTENTS

CONTENTS

FEAR

Fearlessness

Most of us experience a life full of wonderful moments and difficult moments. But for many of us, even when we are most joyful, there is fear behind our joy. We fear that this moment will end, that we won't get what we need, that we will lose what we love, or that we will not be safe. Often, our biggest fear is the knowledge that one day our bodies will cease functioning. So even when we are surrounded by all the conditions for happiness, our joy is not complete.

We think that, to be happier, we should push away or ignore our fear. We don't feel at ease when we think of the things that scare us, so we deny our fear away. "Oh, no, I don't want to think about that." We try to ignore our fear, but it is still there.

The only way to ease our fear and be truly happy is to acknowledge our fear and look deeply at its source. Instead of trying to escape from our fear, we can invite it up to our awareness and look at it clearly and deeply.

We are afraid of things outside of ourselves that we cannot control. We worry about becoming ill, aging, and losing the things we treasure most. We try to hold tight to the things we care about—our positions, our property, our loved ones. But holding tightly doesn't ease our fear. Eventually, one day, we will have to let go of all of them. We cannot take them with us.

We may think that if we ignore our fears, they'll go away. But if we bury worries and anxieties in our consciousness, they continue to affect us and bring us more sorrow. We are very afraid of being powerless. But we have the power to look deeply at our fears, and then fear cannot control us. We can transform our fear. The practice of living fully in the present moment—what we call *mindfulness*—can give us the courage to face our fears and no longer be pushed and pulled around by them. To be mindful means to look deeply, to touch our true nature of interbeing and recognize that nothing is ever lost.

One day during the Vietnam War, I was sitting in a vacant airfield in the highlands of Vietnam. I was waiting for a plane to go North to study a flooding situation and help bring relief to the flood victims. The situation was urgent, so I had to go in a military plane that was usually used to transport such things as blankets and clothing. I was sitting alone in the airfield waiting for the next plane when an American officer came up to me. He was also waiting for his plane. It was during the war, and there were only the two of us at the airfield. I looked at him and saw that he was young. Immediately, I had a lot of compassion for him. Why does he have to come here to kill or be killed? So out of compassion I said, "You must be very afraid of the Viet Cong." The Viet Cong were Vietnamese communist guerrillas. Unfortunately, I wasn't very skillful, and what I said watered the seed of fear in him. He immediately touched his gun and asked me, "Are you a Viet Cong?"

Before coming to Vietnam, U.S. Army officers had learned that everyone in Vietnam could be a Viet Cong, and fear inhabited every American soldier. Every child, every monk, could be a guerrilla agent. The soldiers had been educated this way, and they saw enemies everywhere. I'd tried to express my sympathy to the soldier, but as soon as he'd heard the word *Viet Cong* he'd been overwhelmed by his fear and went for his gun.

I knew I had to be very calm. I practiced breathing in and breathing out very deeply and then said, "No, I am waiting for my plane to go to Danang to study the flooding and see how I can help." I had a lot of sympathy for him, and this came through in my voice. As we talked, I was able to communicate that I believed the war had created a lot of victims, not only Vietnamese but also Americans. The soldier calmed down as well, and we were able to talk. I was safe, because I had enough lucidity and calm. If I had acted out of fear, he would have shot me out of his fear. So don't think that dangers come only from outside. They come from inside. If we don't acknowledge and look deeply at our own fears, we can draw dangers and accidents to us.

We all experience fear, but if we can look deeply into our fear, we will be able to free ourselves from its grip and touch joy. Fear keeps us focused on the past or worried about the future. If we can acknowledge our fear, we can realize that right now we are okay. Right now, today, we are still alive, and our bodies are working marvelously. Our eyes can still see the beautiful sky. Our ears can still hear the voices of our loved ones.

The first part of looking at our fear is just inviting it into our awareness without judgment. We just acknowledge gently that it is there. This brings a lot of relief already. Then, once our fear has calmed down, we can embrace it tenderly and look deeply into its roots, its sources. Understanding the origins of our anxieties and fears will help us let go of them. Is our fear coming from something that is happening right now, or is it an old fear, a fear from when we were small, that we've kept inside? When we practice inviting all our fears up, we become aware that we are still alive, that we still have many things to treasure and enjoy. If we are not busy pushing down and managing our fear, we can enjoy the sunshine, the fog, the air, and the water. If you can look deeply into your fear and have a clear vision of it, then you really can live a life that is worthwhile.

Our greatest fear is that when we die we will become nothing. To really be free of fear, we must look deeply into the ultimate dimension to see our true nature of no-birth and no-death. We need to free ourselves from these ideas that we are just our bodies, which die. When we understand that we are more than our physical bodies, that we didn't come from nothingness and will not disappear into nothingness, we are liberated from fear.

The Buddha was a human being, and he also knew fear. But because he spent each day practicing mindfulness and looking closely at his fear, when confronted with the unknown, he was able to face it calmly and peacefully. There is a story about a time the Buddha was out walking and Angulimala, a notorious serial killer, came upon him. Angulimala shouted for the Buddha to stop, but the Buddha kept walking slowly and calmly. Angulimala caught up with him and demanded to know why he hadn't stopped. The Buddha replied, "Angulimala, I stopped a long time ago. It is you who have not stopped." He went on to explain, "I stopped committing acts that cause suffering to other living beings. All living beings want to live. All fear death. We must nurture a heart of compassion and protect the lives of all beings." Startled, Angulimala asked to know more. By the end of the conversation, Angulimala vowed never again to commit violent acts and decided to become a monk.

How could the Buddha remain so calm and relaxed when faced with a murderer? This is an extreme example, but each of us faces our fears in one way or another every day. A daily practice of mindfulness can be of enormous help. Beginning with our breath, beginning with awareness, we are able to meet whatever comes our way.

Fearlessness is not only possible, it is the ultimate joy. When you touch nonfear, you are free. If I am ever in an airplane and the pilot announces that the plane is about to crash, I will practice mindful breathing. If you receive bad news, I hope you will do the same. But don't wait for the critical moment to arrive before you start practicing to transform your fear and live mindfully. Nobody can give you fearlessness. Even if the Buddha were sitting right here next to you, he couldn't give it to you. You have to practice and realize it yourself. If you make a habit of mindfulness practice, when difficulties arise, you will already know what to do.

A Time Before

Many of us don't remember this, but a long time ago, we lived inside our mothers' wombs. We were tiny, living human beings. There were two hearts inside your mother's body: her own heart and your heart. During this time your mother did everything for you; she breathed for you, ate for you, drank for you. You were linked to her through your umbilical cord. Oxygen and food came to you through the umbilical cord, and you were safe and content inside of your mother. You were never too hot or too cold. You were very comfortable. You rested on a soft cushion made of water. In China and Vietnam we call the womb the *palace of the child*. You spent about nine months in the palace.

The nine months you spent in the womb were some of the most pleasant times of your life. Then the day of your birth arrived. Everything felt different around you, and you were thrust into a new environment. You felt cold and hunger for the first time. Sounds were too loud; lights were too bright. For the first time, you felt afraid. This is original fear.

Inside the palace of the child you didn't need to use your own lungs. But at the moment of your birth, someone cut the umbilical cord and you were no longer physically joined with your mother. Your mother could no longer breathe for you. You had to learn how to breathe on your own for the first time. If you couldn't breathe on your own, you would die. Birth was an extremely precarious time. You were pushed out of the palace, and you encountered suffering. You tried to inhale, but it was difficult. There was some liquid in your lungs and to breathe in you had to first push out that liquid. We were born, and with that birth, our fear was born along with the desire to survive. This is original desire.

As infants, each one of us knew that to survive, we had to get someone to take care of us. Even after our umbilical cord was cut, we still had to rely entirely on adults to survive. When you depend on someone or something else to survive, it means that a link, a kind of invisible umbilical cord, is still there between you.

When we grow up, our original fear and original desire are still there. Although we are no longer babies, we still fear that we cannot survive, that no one will take care of us. Every desire we will have in our lives has its root in this original, fundamental desire to survive. As babies, we all find ways to ensure our survival. We may have felt very powerless. We had legs but couldn't walk. We had hands but couldn't grasp anything. We had to figure out how to get someone else to protect us, take care of us, and ensure our survival.

Everyone is afraid sometimes. We fear loneliness, being abandoned, growing old, dying, and being sick, among many other things. Sometimes, we may feel fear without knowing exactly why. If we practice looking deeply, we see that this fear is the result of that original fear from the time we were newborns, helpless and unable to do anything for ourselves. Even though we have grown into adults, that original fear and original desire are both still alive. Our desire to have a partner is, in part, a continuation of our desire for someone to take care of us.

As adults, we're often afraid to remember or be in touch with that original fear and desire, because the helpless child in us is still alive. We haven't had a chance to talk to him or her. We haven't taken the time to care for the wounded child, the helpless child within.

For most of us, our original fear continues in some form. Sometimes we might feel scared of being alone. We may feel that "alone I can't make it; I have to have somebody." This is a continuation of our original fear. If we look deeply, however, we will find that we have the capacity to calm our fear and find our own happiness.

We need to look closely at our relationships to see whether they are based primarily on mutual need or on mutual happiness. We have a tendency to think that our partner has the power to make us feel good and that we're not okay unless we have that other person there. We think, "I need this person to take care of me, or I will not survive."

If your relationship is based on fear rather than on mutual understanding and happiness, it doesn't have a solid foundation. You may feel you require that person for your own happiness. And yet at some point you may find the presence of the other person to be a nuisance and want to get rid of him. Then you know for sure that your feelings of peace and security did not really come from that person.

Similarly, if you like to spend a lot of your time at a café, it may not be because that particular café is so interesting. It may be because you're afraid of being alone; you feel that you always have to be with other people. When you turn on the television, it may not be because there's a fascinating program you want to see; it's because you're afraid of being alone with yourself.

If you're afraid of what other people might think of you, it comes from that same place. You're afraid that if others think negatively about you, they won't accept you and you'll be left all alone, in danger. So if you need others to always think well of you, that is a continuation of that same original fear. If you regularly go shopping to buy yourself new clothes, it's because of that same desire; you want to be accepted by others. You're afraid of rejection. You're afraid you'll be abandoned and left alone, with no one to take care of you.

We have to look deeply to identify the original, primal fear and desire that are behind so many of our behaviors. Every one of the fears and desires that you have today is a continuation of original fear and desire.

One day I was walking, and I felt something like an umbilical cord linking me to the sun in the sky. I saw very clearly that if the sun was not there, I would die right away. Then I saw an umbilical cord linking me to the river. I knew that if the river wasn't there, I would also die, because there would be no water for me to drink. And I saw an umbilical cord linking me to the forest. The trees in the forest were creating oxygen for me to breathe. Without the forest, I would die. And I saw an umbilical cord linking me to the farmer who grows the vegetables, wheat, and rice that I cook and eat.

When you practice meditation, you begin to see things that other people do not see. Although you don't see all these umbilical cords, they are there, linking you to your mother, your father, the farmer, the sun, the river, the forest, and so on. Meditation can include visualization. If you were to draw a picture of yourself with these many umbilical cords, you would discover that there are not only five or ten, but maybe hundreds or thousands of them, and you are linked to them all.

In Plum Village, where I live in southwest France, we like to use *gathas*, short practice poems that we recite silently or out loud throughout the day, to help us live deeply every action of our daily life. We have a gatha for waking up in the morning, a gatha for brushing our teeth, and even gathas for using the car or the computer. The gatha we say as we serve our food goes like this:

In this food
I see clearly
the presence of the entire universe
supporting my existence.*

Looking deeply into the vegetables, we see sunshine is inside them, a cloud is inside, the earth is inside, and a lot of hard, loving work is also there in the food before us. Looking in this way, even if no one else is sitting down with us to share that meal, we know that our community, our ancestors, Mother Nature, and the whole cosmos are right there, with us and inside us in every moment. We never need to feel alone.

One of the first things we can do to soothe our fear is to talk to it. You can sit down with that fearful child inside and be gentle with him or her. You might say something like this: "Dear little child, I am your adult self. I would like to tell you that we are no longer a baby, helpless and vulnerable. We have strong hands and strong feet; we can very well defend ourselves. So there is no reason why we have to continue to be fearful anymore."

I believe that talking to the child like that can be very helpful, because the inner child may be deeply wounded, and the child has been waiting for us to come back to her. All her childhood wounds are still there, and we have been

---

* A complete collection of gathas and information on how to practice them in daily life may be found in my book *Peace Is Every Breath*.

so busy that we have had no time to go back and help the child heal. That is why it's very important to take the time to go back, to recognize the presence of the wounded child in us, to talk to him and try to help him heal. We can remind him several times that we are no longer a helpless child, we have grown up into an adult, and we can very well take care of ourselves.

Practice: Talking to Your Inner Child

Put down two cushions. First sit on one cushion and pretend you are the helpless, vulnerable child. You express yourself: "Dear one, I am very helpless. I cannot do anything. It's very dangerous. I'm going to die; nobody is taking care of me." You have to speak the language of the baby. And while you are expressing yourself like that, if the feelings of fear, hopelessness, stress, and helplessness come up, please allow them to come up and recognize them. Allow the helpless child enough time to express herself fully. This is very important.

After she has finished, move to the other cushion to play the role of the adult self. As you look at the other cushion, imagine the helpless child is sitting there and talk to her: "Listen to me. I am your adult self. You are no longer a helpless child; we have grown up into an adult already. We have enough intelligence to protect ourselves, to survive by ourselves. We don't need someone to take care of us anymore."

When you try this, you will see that the feeling of safety and security you want to feel doesn't need to come from clinging to another person or from constantly distracting yourself. Acknowledging and soothing the fear within is the first step in letting it go.

Understanding that we are now safe is essential for those of us who have suffered abuse, fear, or pain in our past. Sometimes we may need a friend, a brother, a sister, a teacher, to help us not fall back into the past. We have grown up. We're now capable not just of defending ourselves but of living fully in the present moment and giving to others.

Original Fear

Many of us often find ourselves thinking of things that stir up feelings of fear and sorrow. We have all experienced some suffering in our past, and we often recall our past suffering. We revisit the past, reviewing it and watching the films of the past. But if we revisit these memories without mindfulness or awareness, every time we watch those images we suffer again.

Suppose you were abused as a young child. You suffered greatly. You were fragile and vulnerable. You were likely afraid all the time. You didn't know how to protect yourself. Perhaps in your mind you continue to be abused again and again, even though you are an adult now. You are no longer that child who was fragile and vulnerable, with no means of defense. Yet you continue to experience the suffering of the child, because you always revisit those memories even though they are painful.

There is a film, an image stored in your consciousness. Every time your mind goes back to the past and you look at that image or watch that film, you suffer again. Mindfulness reminds us that it is possible to be in the here and now. It reminds us that the present moment is always available to us; we don't have to live events that happened long ago.

Suppose someone slapped your face twenty years ago. That was recorded as an image in your subconscious. Your subconscious stores many films and images of the past, which are always being projected down there. And you have a tendency to go back and watch them again and again, so you continue to suffer. Every time you see that picture, you are slapped again and again and again.

But that is only the past. You are no longer in the past; you are in the present moment. That *did* happen, yes—in the past. But the past is already gone. Now the only things left are pictures and memories. If you keep going back to the past to review those images, that is wrong mindfulness. But if we root ourselves in the present moment, we can look at the past in a different way and transform its suffering.

Perhaps when you were a little child, people would sometimes take your toy away from you. You learned to cry, to try to manipulate the situation; or to smile so as to please your caretaker, to make her give back the toy. As a young child, you learned to produce a diplomatic smile. That's one way of dealing with the problem of survival. You learn without even knowing that you're learning. The feeling that you're fragile, vulnerable, unable to defend yourself, the feeling that you always need someone to be with you, is always there. That original fear—and its other face, original desire—is always there. The infant, with his fear and his desire, is always alive in us.

Some of us have depression and continue to suffer even if in the present situation everything looks all right. This is because we have a tendency to dwell in the past. We feel more comfortable making our home there, even if it holds a lot of suffering. That home is deep down in our subconscious, where the films of the past are always projected. Every night you go back and watch those films and suffer. And the future you constantly worry about is nothing other than a projection of fear and desire from the past.

Don't Fear the Past

Because it's so easy to be caught in the past, it's helpful to have a reminder to stay in the present. In Plum Village, we use a bell. When we hear the bell, we practice breathing in and out mindfully, and we say, "I listen to the bell. This wonderful sound brings me back to my true home." My true home is in the here and now. The past is not my true home.

You may want to say to the little one inside you, the past is not our home; our home is here, where we can really live our life. We can get all the nourishment and healing we need here in the present moment. Much of the fear, anxiety, and anguish that we experience is there because the inner child has not been liberated. That child is afraid to come out to the present moment, and so your mindfulness, your breath, can help this child to realize that she is safe and can be free.

Suppose you go to the movies. From your seat in the audience you look up at the screen. There is a story; there are people on the screen interacting with each other. And down there in the audience, you cry. You experience what's happening on the screen as real, and that's why you shed real tears and feel real emotions. The suffering is real; the tears are real. But when you come up to touch the screen, you don't see any real people. It's nothing but flickering light. You can't talk to the people on the screen; you can't invite them to have tea. You can't stop them or ask them a question, but yet it can create real suffering, in your body as well as your mind. Our memories can cause us real suffering, both emotionally and physically, even though they are not happening in the moment.

When we recognize that we have a habit of replaying old events and reacting to new events as if they were the old ones, we can begin to notice when that habit energy comes up. We can then gently remind ourselves that we have another choice. We can look at the moment as it is, a fresh moment, and leave the past for a time when we can look at it compassionately.

We can make the time and space, not in a busy moment but in a quiet time, to tell the suffering, wounded child inside us that she doesn't have to suffer anymore. We can take her hand and invite her to come into the present moment and witness all the wonders of life that are available here and now: "Come with me, dear one. We have grown up. We no longer need to be afraid. We are no longer vulnerable. We are no longer fragile. We don't have to be afraid anymore."

You have to teach the child in you. You have to invite him to come with you and live life with you in the present moment. Of course, we can mindfully reflect upon and learn from the past, but when we do this we stay grounded in the present moment. If we are well grounded in the present moment, we can look skillfully at the past and learn from it without being sucked in and overwhelmed by it.

Contemplating the Future Without Fear

We likewise can prepare for the future without getting consumed by our plans. Often we either don't plan at all, or we get caught up in obsessive planning because we fear the future and its uncertainty. The present moment is where we need to operate. When you are truly anchored in the present moment, you can plan for the future in a much better way. Living mindfully in the present does not preclude making plans. It only means that you know there's no use losing yourself in worries and fear concerning the future. If you are grounded in the present moment, you can bring the future into the present to have a deep look without losing yourself in anxiety and uncertainty. If you are truly present and know how to take care of the present moment as best you can, you are doing your best for the future already.

The same is true about the past. The teaching and the practice of mindfulness do not forbid looking deeply into the past. But if we allow ourselves to drown in regret and sorrow concerning the past, that's not right mindfulness. If we're well established in the present moment, we can bring the past back to the present moment and have a deep look. You can very well examine the past and the future while you are established in the present moment. In fact you can learn from the past and plan for the future in the best way if you are grounded in the present moment.

If you have a friend who suffers, you have to help him. "My dear friend, you are on safe ground. Everything is okay now. Why do you continue to suffer? Don't go back to the past. It's only a ghost; it's unreal." And whenever we recognize that these are only movies and pictures, not reality, we are free. That is the practice of mindfulness.

Reconciling with Our Past

Our original fear isn't just from our own birth and childhood; the fear we feel comes from both our own and our ancestors' original fear. Our ancestors suffered from hunger and other dangers, and there were moments when they were extremely anxious. That kind of fear has been transmitted to us; every one of us has that fear inside. And because we suffer from that fear, we make the situation worse. We worry about our safety, our job, and our family. We worry about external threats. Even when nothing bad is happening, that doesn't prevent us from feeling fear.

Once, a young American came to Plum Village and practiced meditation with several others. During this time, I suggested to everyone present that they write a love letter to a parent, regardless of whether that parent was still living. Writing a letter is a form of meditation practice. This young man could not do it, because every time he thought of his father he suffered greatly. His father had already died, and yet he could not reconcile with him. His father had terrified him when he was growing up, so much so that even now he was afraid to speak to him through a letter. He could not bear to even think of his father, much less write to him. So I gave him an exercise to practice for one week: "Breathing in, I see myself as a five-year-old child. Breathing out, I smile to that five-year-old child."

When you are a small boy or girl, you are very fragile, very vulnerable. Just a stern look from your father can create a little wound in your heart. If your father tells you to shut up, you can get wounded. You are very tender. Sometimes you want to express yourself, you try very hard to find words, and your father is a little irritated and he says, "Shut up." It is like a bowl of ice water being poured on your heart. It wounds you deeply, and the next time you will not dare to try again. Your communication with your father becomes very difficult. "Breathing in I see myself as a five-year-old child. Breathing out I smile to that five-year-old child."

Do you think that child is no longer there? The little boy or girl in you is still alive, and maybe still deeply wounded. That child is calling for your attention. But you have no time for him or her. You're too busy. You conceive of yourself as an adult, but in fact, you are also that little girl or boy who is deeply wounded and afraid. So when you breathe in and see yourself as a small child who is fragile like that, compassion is born in your heart. And when you breathe out, you smile to him or her, and that is already a smile of understanding, of compassion.

The little child inside you can suffer so much. When you were small, you were deeply affected by the decisions adults made around you. A child is very impressionable. Even before he or she is born, a child hears sounds and can distinguish shouting from singing. This is why, if you really care for your child, even when your child is not yet born, you will surround that child with love. Love should begin very early.

There are many young people who say they hate their fathers or mothers. They sometimes tell me, in strong, clear terms: "I don't want to have anything to do with him, with her." These people are so angry with their parents that they want to completely sever the relationship. Sometimes, people have good reasons for separating themselves physically or emotionally from their parents, especially if their parents are abusive. Sometimes, we fear that if we are around our parents, we will be too vulnerable and will get hurt again.

But even if we refuse to see our parents or talk to them, we cannot separate ourselves completely from them. We are made from them. We are our fathers. We are our mothers. This is true even if we think we hate them.

We are the continuation of our mothers and fathers. We can't extract that part of ourselves. To get angry with our parents doesn't change this. We are only getting angry with ourselves. We need to reconcile with the parents inside, talk to the parents inside, and look for a way to peacefully coexist. If we can realize this, reconciliation will be easy.

We are capable of great change, both internally and also in our ability to influence the world outside us. Because we are scared, we often think we don't know what to do. But we only need to practice mindful walking and mindful breathing, to cultivate the energy of mindfulness and understanding. Understanding, when it comes, helps us release our fear, our anger, our hate, and so on. Love can only be born on the ground of understanding.

When we say that body and mind are connected, this does not mean just your own individual body and mind. In you are all your blood ancestors and also your spiritual ancestors. You can touch the presence of your father and mother in each cell of your body. They are truly present in you, along with your grandparents and great-grandparents. Doing this, you know you are their continuation. You may have thought that your ancestors no longer existed, but even scientists say your ancestors are present in you, in the genetic heritage that is in every cell of your body. The same is true for your descendants. You will be present in every cell of their bodies. And you are present in the consciousness of everyone you have touched.

Think of a plum tree. In each plum on the tree there is a pit. That pit contains the plum tree and all previous generations of plum tree. The plum pit contains an infinite number of plum trees. Inside the pit is an intelligence, a wisdom that knows how to become a plum tree, how to produce branches, leaves, flowers, and plums. It cannot do this on its own. It can do this only because it has received the experience and adaptations of so many generations of ancestors. You are the same. You possess the wisdom and intelligence to become a full human being because you have inherited an eternity of wisdom, not only from your blood ancestors but from your spiritual ancestors too.

Your spiritual ancestors are in you because what you are by nature and what you are by nurture cannot be separated. Nurturing transforms your inherited nature. Your spirituality and your mindfulness practice, which are parts of your daily life, are also in every cell of your body. So your spiritual ancestors are in every cell of your body. You cannot deny their presence.

Some of us have wonderful parents; others have parents who suffered a lot and made their partners and their children suffer. Just about everyone has some blood ancestors whom we admire, and others who had many negative traits and of whom we are not proud. They are all our ancestors. We may also have spiritual ancestors who did not help us and may even have done harm. We may be angry with them, but they are still our ancestors.

We need to return to ourselves and embrace our blood and spiritual ancestors. We cannot get rid of them. They are a reality and they are there inside us, in body, mind, and spirit. Unconditional acceptance is the first step in opening the door to the miracle of forgiveness.

Practice: Accepting Our Ancestors

To sincerely accept others as they are, we must begin with ourselves. If we cannot accept ourselves as we are, we will never be able to accept others. When I look at myself, I see positive, admirable, and even remarkable things, but I also know that there are negative parts of me. So first I recognize and accept myself.

Breathing in and breathing out, you visualize your ancestors, and you see all their positive and negative points. Be determined to accept them all as your ancestors without hesitation.

> *Dear ancestors, I am you, with all your strengths and weaknesses. I see you have negative and positive seeds. I understand that you have been lucky and that good seeds like kindness, compassion, and fearlessness were watered in you. I also understand that if you were not lucky and negative seeds like fear, greed, and jealousy were watered in you, then the positive seeds did not have a chance to grow.*

When a person's positive seeds are watered in life, it is partly because of luck and partly because of effort. The circumstances of our lives can help us water the seeds of patience, generosity, compassion, and love. The people around us can help us water these seeds, and so can the practice of mindfulness. But if a person grows up in a time of war or in a family and community that is suffering, that person may be full of despair and fear. Parents who suffer a lot and are afraid of the world and other people water the seeds of fear and anger in their children. If children grow up embraced by security and love, the good seeds in them are nurtured and grow strong.

If you can look at your ancestors in this way, you will understand that they were human beings who suffered and tried their best. That understanding will erase all rejection and anger. Accepting all your ancestors with both their strengths and their weaknesses will help you become more peaceful and less afraid. You can also see your elder brothers and sisters as your (youngest) ancestors, because they were born before you. They too have strengths and challenges, like all of us.

Making peace with your ancestors takes some practice, but it is important to reconcile with them if you are to settle the fear within yourself. You can do this anywhere, before an altar or a tree, on a mountain, or in the city. All you need to do is visualize the presence of all your ancestors inside you. You are their continuation. Only when you make your peace with them can you be one hundred percent in the moment.

Releasing Fears About the Future

The Five Remembrances

In addition to getting caught in dwelling on events that happened in the past, we often walk around in fear of what will happen to us in the future. The fear of death is one of the greatest fears people have. When we look directly into the seeds of this fear instead of trying to cover it up or run away, we begin to transform it. One of the most powerful ways to do this is with the practice of the five remembrances. If you breathe slowly and mindfully, in and out, deep and slow, while you say these remembrances to yourself, it will help you look deeply into the nature and roots of your fear.

The five remembrances are:

1. I am of the nature to grow old. I cannot escape growing old.

2. I am of the nature to have ill health. I cannot escape having ill health.

3. I am of the nature to die. I cannot escape death.

4. All that is dear to me, and everyone I love, are of the nature to change. There is no way to escape being separated from them.

5. I inherit the results of my acts of body, speech, and mind. My actions are my continuation.

Looking deeply at each remembrance and breathing in and out with our awareness of each one, we engage our fear in an empowered way.

I am of the nature to grow old. I cannot escape growing old.

That is the first remembrance: "Breathing in, I know I am of the nature to grow old. Breathing out, I know I can't escape growing old." We are all afraid of getting old. We don't want to think about it. We want that fear to stay peacefully down there, far away from us. This contemplation comes from the sutra in the Anguttara Nikaya III 70–71. *Surely I will have to grow old*. This is a truth that is universal and inevitable. But most of us don't want to acknowledge it, so we live more or less in denial. Yet down deep in the recesses of our minds, we know it's true. When we suppress our fearful thoughts, they continue to fester there in the dark. We are driven to consume (food, alcohol, movies, etc.) in an attempt to forget and keep those thoughts from surfacing in our conscious mind. Running away from our fear ultimately makes us suffer and makes others suffer, and our fear only grows stronger.

We must be able to accept this as reality, as the truth, and not just as a logical fact. Reciting this remembrance is not mere restatement of the obvious but a chance to take in a truth that we need to experience directly. We can take a few moments to let that truth penetrate into our flesh and bones. We shouldn't just leave it to our intellectual understanding ("Yes, yes of course, now I'm young, but one day I'll get old"). That's just an abstract notion that brings no benefit, especially since our mind usually works to repress and forget about it right away after we say it.

The Buddha taught that when we call up and get in touch with the truth that we cannot escape old age and death, our fear—and the foolish things we do to try not to feel it—will cease. We no longer act out our fears unconsciously and fuel the cycle that makes them grow ever stronger.

I am of the nature to have ill health.
I cannot escape having ill health.

The second remembrance recognizes that sickness is a universal phenomenon: "Breathing in, I know I am of the nature to have ill health. Breathing out, I know I can't escape having ill health." Siddhartha, as the Buddha was called before he practiced and became enlightened, was one of the strongest young men in Kapilavastu. He often took first place in sporting contests, and everyone, including his envious cousin Devadatta, dreamed of having Siddhartha's prowess. Siddhartha naturally became arrogant, knowing that few people were as strong as he. But when he practiced looking deeply in sitting meditation, Siddhartha recognized his arrogance and was able to let go of it.

If we are in normal good health, we may think getting sick is for other people. We look down on others, saying they're always getting sick from nothing at all; they have to take medicine and receive massage all the time. We think we're not like them.

But one day we will likely also fall sick. If we are not diligent in contemplating this reality now, then when that day suddenly comes upon us we won't be able to handle it. Our legs are still strong now; we can run, do walking meditation, play soccer. We can still use our arms to do many things. But most of us aren't making good use of our ability to take good care of others and ourselves. We don't use our energy for the practice of transforming our afflictions and helping to relieve suffering in others and ourselves.

One day, we'll be lying down on the bed, and even if we want nothing more than just to stand up and take one step, we won't be able to do it. That's why we must see right in the present moment that, having a body, surely we will get sick one day. Seeing this, naturally we will drop our arrogance about our good health. The path of right conduct will appear; we will make good use of our time and energy to do what's needed and not be carried away by senseless pursuits that can destroy our bodies and minds. What we need to do will become clear.

I am of the nature to die. I cannot escape death.

This is the third remembrance: "Breathing in, I know it is my nature to die. Breathing out, I know I can't escape dying." It's a simple and true fact that you are reluctant to face. You want this fact to get lost, because you're afraid. It's painful for you to look deeply into it. Death is a reality that we have to confront. The subconscious mind is always trying to forget that, because when we touch that fear and we are not equipped with the energy of mindfulness, we suffer. Our defense mechanism pushes us to forget; we don't want to hear about it. But in the back of our minds, the fear of death is always there, pushing on us.

When we really face the fact that we will die one day (and maybe sooner than we think), we won't embarrass ourselves doing ridiculous things, keeping up the delusion that we're going to live forever. Contemplating our mortality helps us focus our energy into the practice of transforming and healing ourselves and our world.

All that is dear to me, and everyone I love, are of the nature to change. There is no way to escape being separated from them.

This is the fourth remembrance: "Breathing in, I know that one day I will have to let go of everything and everyone I love. Breathing out, there is no way to bring them along." Everything that I cherish today I will have to leave behind tomorrow, whether it is my house, my bank account, my children, or my beautiful partner. Everything that I cherish today, I will have to abandon. I cannot carry anything with me when I die. This is a scientific truth. What we cherish, what belongs to us today, won't be there tomorrow; we will have to take leave not only of our most cherished objects but also of the people we love.

We can't take anything or anyone else with us in our death. Yet every day we strive to accumulate more and more money, knowledge, fame, and everything else. Even when we reach sixty or seventy years of age, we keep grasping for more knowledge, money, fame, and power. We know that the mementos and belongings we covet must all be abandoned one day. That's why those in monastic life practice not to collect things. The Buddha said monastics should have only three robes, a begging bowl, a water filter, and a sitting mat, and even these few things they also should be prepared to release. The Buddha often said that we should not be attached to even the foot of that tree where we like to sit and sleep. We should be able to sit and sleep at the foot of any tree. Our happiness should not depend on having that particular spot. We must be ready to let go.

If we practice and are able to release, we can be free and happy right now, today. If we can't let go, we will suffer not only on the day when we're finally forced to do so, but right now today and every day in between, because fear will be constantly stalking us. There are old people who are still very greedy and stingy, like Scrooge, continuing to hoard everything. This is a shame. It's not because they're not smart enough to see that someday soon, maybe in just a few months, they'll have to let go of everything. It's because covetousness has become a habit; throughout their lives they've been seeking happiness in accumulating things. Even just three months before they pass away, that habit is still strong and prevents them from letting go.

There's a Vietnamese legend about a rich man named Thach Sung who was very proud because his storehouse had everything that could be found in the king's storehouse. He congratulated himself for having as much gold and treasure as the king himself, maybe even more. The king asked Thach Sung one day whether he was sure he was the richer man.

Thach Sung was so sure of himself, he wagered that if there was anything in the king's storehouse that wasn't in his own storehouse, he would give everything he owned to the king. This is the arrogance of wealth. With the king's ministers witnessing, the challenge began. Indeed, everything the king displayed, Thach Sung also had. But at the end of the day there was one thing the king had that Thach Sung didn't have: a broken cooking pot! That broken cooking pot couldn't be used to make soup but could be used to make fish or tofu dishes. The minister of justice declared that Thach Sung had lost his wager. Thach Sung had to deliver on his vow and give all his property to the king. He was so upset that he turned into a lizard, always clicking his tongue, "Tsk, tsk! Tsk, tsk!"

We don't want to become Thach Sung, searching for happiness in the accumulation of material things. The Buddha once told the monastics to look up at the sky at night to see the moon, and he asked them whether they saw how great the moon's happiness was as it traveled in the vast open space. As practitioners we should allow ourselves to be as free as the moon. If we are attached to obtaining more and more wealth, fame, power, and sex, we lose our freedom.

I inherit the results of my acts
of body, speech, and mind.
My actions are my continuation.

The fifth remembrance reminds us that when we die, the only things that continue us are our thoughts, words, and actions—that is, our karma. "Breathing in, I know that I bring nothing with me except my thoughts, words, and deeds. Breathing out, only my actions come with me." All the thoughts you have thought, all the words you have spoken, all the actions you have done with your body—these are your karma that follows and continues you. Everything else you leave behind.

Here we are speaking of inheriting not our parents' savings, but the fruits of our own actions. What we have thought, said, and done is called *karma,* which in Sanskrit means action. What we do, say, and think continues on after the act is done, and its fruits follow us. Whether we want that inheritance or not, it stays with us. All our cherished belongings and loved ones we must leave behind, but our karma, the fruit of our actions, always follows us. We never can escape it; we never can say, "No! You have no right to pursue me!" Karma is the ground on which we stand. We have only one foundation, and that is our karma. We have no other ground. We will receive the fruits of any act we have done, whether wholesome or unwholesome.

Bringing Mindfulness to the Seeds of Fear

The practice of the five remembrances helps us accept many of our deepest fears—such as old age, sickness, and death—as realities, facts we cannot escape. When we practice accepting these truths, we can realize peace and have the capacity to live conscious, healthy, and compassionate lives, no longer causing suffering to ourselves and others.

Invite your fear into consciousness, and smile through it; every time you smile through your fear, it will lose some of its strength. If you try to run away from your pain, there is no way out. Only by looking deeply into the nature of your fear can you find the way out.

Contemplating the five remembrances, we bring mindfulness to the seed of fear in us. The seed of fear is there in us, and if we don't practice embracing it with mindfulness, then every time these truths show themselves, we will feel very uncomfortable. Like ostriches that see a lion, we stick our heads in the sand. Using diversions like television, computer games, alcohol, and drugs, we try to ignore the realities of aging, illness, death, and the impermanence of the things we cherish.

If we allow ourselves to be overwhelmed by our fears, we will suffer, and the seed of fear in us will grow stronger. But when we are mindful, we use the energy of mindfulness to embrace our fear. Every time fear is embraced by mindfulness, the energy of fear decreases before going back down to the depths of our consciousness as a seed.

Our consciousness is like a circle in which the bottom part is our store consciousness and the upper part is our mind consciousness. The fear of aging, the fear of illness, the fear of death, the fear of having to let go, and the fear of the consequences of our karma are all there in our store consciousness. We don't want to face our fear, so we try to cover it up, keep it down there in the cellar. We don't like it when somebody or something reminds us of it. We don't want it showing itself in our mind consciousness.

Mindfulness is the opposite of this tendency. We must invite these things up into our mind consciousness every day and tell them, "My dear, I'm not afraid of you. I'm not afraid of my fear. It is my nature to grow old; I cannot escape old age." When fear manifests, we want to have the seed of mindfulness also manifest to embrace it. So we have two energies present—the first is the energy of fear, and the second is the energy of mindfulness. The fear receives a bath of mindfulness and becomes a little bit weaker before it drops back down to the depths of our consciousness in the form of a seed.

Just because fear goes away for a little while doesn't mean we have dissolved it completely. If we have a peaceful moment, a moment of meditation, we can call it up again. "My dear fear, come up here so I can embrace you for a while. It is my nature to die; I cannot escape death." We can stay with our fear for five, ten, twenty, or thirty minutes, depending on our needs, and use the energy of mindfulness to embrace our fear. Being embraced like that every day, our fear will lose its strength.

No Coming,
No Going

Our greatest fear is that when we die, we will become nothing. Many of us believe our entire existence is limited to a particular period, our "lifespan." We believe it begins when we are born—when, out of being nothing, we become something— and it ends when we die and become nothing again. So we are filled with a fear of annihilation.

But if we look deeply, we can have a very different understanding of our existence. We can see that birth and death are just notions; they're not real. The Buddha taught that there is no birth and no death. Our belief that these ideas about birth and death are real creates a powerful illusion that causes us a great deal of suffering. When we understand that we can't be destroyed, we're liberated from fear. It's a huge relief. We can enjoy life and appreciate it in a new way.

When I lost my mother, I suffered a lot. The day she died, I wrote in my journal, "The greatest misfortune of my life has happened." I grieved her death for more than a year. Then one night, I was sleeping in my hermitage—a hut that lay behind a temple, halfway up a hill covered with tea plants in the highlands of Vietnam. I had a dream about my mother. I saw myself sitting with her, and we were having a wonderful talk. She looked young and beautiful, with her hair flowing down around her shoulders. It was so pleasant to sit and talk to her as if she had never died.

When I woke up, I had a very strong feeling that I had never lost my mother. The sense that my mother was still with me was very clear. I understood then that the idea of having lost my mother was just that: an idea. It was obvious in that moment that my mother was still alive in me and always would be.

I opened the door and went outside. The entire hillside was bathed in moonlight. Walking slowly in that soft light through the rows of tea plants, I observed that my mother was indeed still with me. My mother was the moonlight caressing me as she had so often done, very gentle, very sweet. Every time my feet touched the earth, I knew my mother was there with me. I knew this body was not mine alone but a living continuation of my mother and father, my grandparents and great-grandparents, and of all my ancestors. These feet I saw as "my" feet were actually "our" feet. Together my mother and I were leaving footprints in the damp soil.

From that moment on, the idea that I had lost my mother no longer existed. All I had to do was look at the palm of my hand, or feel the breeze on my face or the earth under my feet, to remember that my mother is always with me, available at any time.

When you lose a loved one, you suffer. But if you know how to look deeply, you have a chance to realize that his or her nature is truly the nature of no-birth, no-death. There is manifestation, and there is the cessation of manifestation in order to have another manifestation. You have to be alert to recognize the new manifestations of one person. But with practice and effort, you can do it. Pay attention to the world around you, to the leaves and the flowers, to the birds and the rain. If you can stop and look deeply, you will recognize your beloved manifesting again and again in many forms. You will release your fear and pain and again embrace the joy of life.

The Present Is Free from Fear

When we are not fully present, we are not really living. We're not really there, either for our loved ones or for ourselves. If we're not there, then where are we? We are running, running, running, even during our sleep. We run because we're trying to escape from our fear.

We cannot enjoy life if we spend our time and energy worrying about what happened yesterday and what will happen tomorrow. If we're afraid all the time, we miss out on the wonderful fact that we're alive and can be happy right now. In everyday life, we tend to believe that happiness is only possible in the future. We're always looking for the "right" conditions that we don't yet have to make us happy. We ignore what is happening right in front of us. We look for something that will make us feel more solid, more safe, more secure. But we're afraid all the time of what the future will bring—afraid we'll lose our jobs, our possessions, the people around us whom we love. So we wait and hope for that magical moment—always sometime in the future—when everything will be as we want it to be. We forget that life is available only in the present moment. The Buddha said, "It is possible to live happily in the present moment. It is the only moment we have."

Buried Treasure

The Bible tells the story of a farmer who discovered a treasure buried on his land. When he went back home, he gave up all the rest of his land and everything else he owned. He kept only that one small piece of land that contained the treasure. That treasure is the kingdom of God. We know that we should look for the kingdom of God in the present moment, because the present moment is the only moment that *is*. The past is gone, and the future is not yet here. So the place where you should look for the kingdom of God or the Pure Land of the Buddha, the place where you should look for your happiness, your peace, and your fulfillment, has to be in the present moment. It's so simple and clear. But since we have the tendency to slide back into the past or to run into the future, we have to recognize that habit and learn how to be free from it to really establish ourselves in the present moment.

When the Buddha gave a talk to a large gathering of businessmen, the core of his message to them was, "It is possible to live happily right in the present moment." The Buddha saw that most of the businessmen were very concerned about their future success and weren't capable of enjoying the present moment. They didn't have time for themselves or their families; they didn't have time to love and make the people around them happy. They were continually being sucked into the future.

The Pure Land is in the present moment. The Pure Land is now or never. The same is true with the kingdom of God: it's either now or never. The kingdom of God is not just a lovely idea. It is a reality. When you do mindful breathing and walking, you go home to the present moment, and you touch the many wonders of life in you and around you; and all of that belongs to the kingdom of God. If you have found the kingdom of God, you no longer need to run after fame and riches and sensual pleasures.

When we go home to the present moment, we understand there are so many conditions of happiness that we don't need to go running after yet another one. We already have enough conditions to be happy. Happiness is entirely possible right in the here and now.

The Buddha's teaching about living happily in the present moment is a very pleasant one. We can be happy right now.

The practice is also very pleasant. When we climb the hill together, we don't need to make an effort; we enjoy every step. Walking like that, if we are free of the past, free of the future, we can touch the kingdom of God, the Pure Land of the Buddha, with every step.

The Here and Now

I have arrived, I am home
In the here, in the now
I am solid, I am free
In the ultimate I dwell

When we come back to the here and now, we recognize the many conditions of happiness that already exist. The practice of mindfulness is the practice of coming back to the here and now to be deeply in touch with ourselves and with life. We have to train ourselves to do this. Even if we're very intelligent and grasp the principle right away, we still have to train ourselves to really live this way. We have to train ourselves to recognize the many conditions for happiness that are already here.

You can recite the poem above as you breathe in and out. You can practice this poem when you drive to your office. You may not have arrived at your office, but even while driving you have already arrived at your true home, the present moment.

When you arrive at your office, this is also your true home. In your office, you are also in the here and now. Just practicing the first line of the poem, "I have arrived, I am home," can make you very happy. Whether you are sitting, walking, watering the vegetable garden, or feeding your child, it is always possible to practice "I have arrived, I am home." I have run all my life; I am not going to run anymore; now I am determined to stop and really live my life.

When we practice breathing in and we say, "I have arrived," and we really arrive, that is success. To be fully present, one hundred percent alive, is a real achievement. The present moment has become our true home. When we breathe out and say, "I am home" and we really feel at home, we no longer have to be afraid. We really don't need to run anymore.

We repeat this mantra, "I have arrived, I am home," until it feels real. We repeat breathing in and out and taking steps until we are firmly established in the here and now. The words should not be an obstacle—the words only help you concentrate and keep your insight alive. It is the insight that keeps you home, not the words.

The Two Dimensions of Reality

If you have succeeded in arriving at home, truly dwelling in the here and now, you already have the solidity and freedom that are the foundation of your happiness. Then you are able to see the two dimensions of reality, the historical and the ultimate.

To represent the two dimensions of reality, we use the images of the wave and water. Looking at the dimension of the wave, the historical dimension, we see that the wave seems to have a beginning and an end. The wave can be high or low compared to other waves. The wave might be more or less beautiful than other waves. The wave might be there or not there; it might be there now but not there later. All these notions are there when we first touch the historical dimension: birth and death, being and nonbeing, high and low, coming and going, and so on. But we know that when we touch the wave more deeply, we touch water. The water is the other dimension of the wave. It represents the ultimate dimension.

In the historical dimension, we talk in terms of life, death, being, nonbeing, high, low, coming, going, but in the ultimate dimension, all these notions are removed. If the wave is capable of touching the water within herself, if the wave can live the life of water at the same time, then she will not be afraid of all these notions: beginning and ending, birth and death, being or nonbeing; nonfear will bring her solidity and joy. Her true nature is the nature of no-birth and no-death, no beginning and no end. That is the nature of water.

All of us are like that wave. We have our historical dimension. We speak in terms of beginning to be at a certain point in time, and ceasing to be at another point in time. We believe that we are now existing and that before our birth we did not exist. We get caught in these notions, and that is why we have fear, we have jealousy, we have craving, we have all these conflicts and afflictions within us. Now if we are capable of arriving, of being more solid and free, it will be possible for us to touch our true nature, the ultimate dimension of ourselves. In touching that ultimate dimension, we break free from all these notions that have made us suffer.

When fear loses some of its power, we can look deeply into its origin from the perspective of the ultimate dimension. In the historical dimension, we see birth, death, and old age, but in the ultimate dimension birth and death are not the true nature of things. The true nature of things is free from birth and death. The first step is to practice in the historical dimension, and the second step is to practice in the ultimate dimension. In the first step we accept that birth and death are happening, but in the second step, because we're in touch with the ultimate dimension, we realize that birth and death come from our own conceptual minds and not from any true reality. By being in contact with the ultimate dimension, we are able to be in touch with the reality of all things, which is birthless and deathless.

Practicing in the historical dimension is very important for our success practicing in the ultimate dimension. Practice in the ultimate dimension means being in touch with our no-birth, no-death nature, like a wave being in touch with its true nature of water. We can ask metaphorically, "Where does the wave come from, and where will it go?" And we can answer in the same manner, "The wave comes from water and will return to water." In reality, there is no coming and going. The wave is always water; it doesn't "come from" water, and it doesn't go anywhere. It is always water; coming and going are just mental constructions. The wave has never left the water, so to say the wave "comes from" the water is not really correct. As it is always water, we cannot say it "returns to" water. Right at the moment when the wave is a wave, it is already water. Birth and death, coming and going, are just concepts. When we are in touch with our no-birth, no-death nature, we have no fear.

The Nature of No-Birth and No-Death

The cloud cannot become nothing. It is possible for a cloud to become rain or snow or hail. But it's not possible for a cloud to become nothing. That's why the view of annihilation is a wrong view. If you're a scientist and you think that after the disintegration of this body you are no longer there—you become nothing, you pass from being to nonbeing—then you are not a very good scientist, because your view goes against the evidence.

So birth and death are paired notions, like coming and going, permanence and annihilation, self and other. The cloud appearing in the sky is a new manifestation. Before assuming the form of a cloud, the cloud was water vapor, produced from water in the ocean and the heat of sunlight. You can call it her previous life. So being a cloud is only a continuation. A cloud has not come from nothing. A cloud always comes from something. So there is no birth; there is only a continuation. That is the nature of everything: no-birth, no-death.

The eighteenth-century French scientist Antoine Lavoisier declared, "Rien ne se crée, rien ne se perd" (Nothing is created, nothing is lost). Lavoisier saw the same truth that the Buddha saw, that nothing is born and nothing dies. Our true nature is no-birth and no-death. Only when we touch our true nature can we transcend the fear of nonbeing, the fear of annihilation.

When conditions are sufficient, something manifests, and we say that it exists. When one or two conditions are no longer there and the thing is not manifesting in the same way, we say that it does not exist. To qualify something as existing or not existing is not correct. In reality, there is no such thing as totally existing or totally not existing.

No Coming, No Going

For many of us, these notions of birth and death, coming and going, cause our greatest pain. We think the person we loved came to us from somewhere and has now gone away somewhere. But our true nature is the nature of no coming and no going. We have not come from anywhere, and we will not go anywhere. When conditions are sufficient, we manifest in a particular way. When conditions are no longer sufficient, we no longer manifest in that way. This doesn't mean that we don't exist. If we're afraid of death, it's because we don't understand that things do not really die.

There's a tendency for people to think that they can eliminate what they don't want: they can burn down a village, they can kill a person. But destroying someone doesn't reduce that person to nothing. They killed Mahatma Gandhi. They shot Martin Luther King Jr. But these people are still among us today. They continue to exist in many forms. Their spirit goes on. Therefore, when we look deeply into our self—into our body, our feelings, and our perceptions—when we look into the mountains, the rivers, or another person, we have to be able to see and touch the nature of no-birth and no-death in them. This is one of the most important practices in the Buddhist tradition.

Impermanence

According to Buddhist wisdom, the view of immortality, or permanence, is a wrong view. Everything is impermanent; everything is changing. Nothing can be the same forever. So permanence is not the true nature of anything. But to say that when we die there is nothing left is a wrong view too.

Immortality and annihilation are also paired opposites. Immortality is a wrong view, because so far we have not seen anything like that. Everything we observe is impermanent, always changing. But annihilation is also a wrong view.

Suppose we speak of the death of a cloud. You look up in the sky and don't see your beloved cloud anymore, and you cry, "O my beloved cloud, you are no longer there. How can I survive without you?" And you weep. You are thinking of the cloud as having passed from being into nonbeing, from existence into nonexistence.

But the truth is, it's impossible for a cloud to die. To die means that from something, you suddenly become nothing at all. To die means that from someone, you suddenly become no one. But we've seen that this is not the case. That's why, when we celebrate someone's birthday, instead of singing "Happy birthday to you," it may be better to sing "Happy continuation day to you." Your birth was not your beginning but only your continuation. You were here already, in other forms.

Let's look at this piece of paper. Before the piece of paper appeared in this form, it was something else. It didn't come from nothing, because from nothing you can't suddenly become something. Looking deeply into the sheet of paper, we can see the trees, the soil, sun, rain, and cloud that nourished the trees, the lumberjack, and the paper mill. You can see the previous life of the sheet of paper. That is where the sheet of paper comes from. Taking the form of a sheet of paper is only its new manifestation; it's not really a birth. So the nature of the sheet of paper is no-birth and no-death.

It's impossible for the sheet of paper to die. When you burn a sheet of paper, you see it transform into smoke, vapor, ash, and heat. The sheet of paper continues in other forms. So to say that after something disintegrates there's nothing left is a wrong view, called the *view of annihilation*.

If we have lost someone who is very close to us and we are grieving her death, we have to look again. That person still continues somehow. And we can do something to help her to continue more beautifully. She is still alive, inside us and around us. Looking in this way, we can still recognize her in different forms, just as we recognize the cloud in our cup of tea. When you drink your cup of tea with mindfulness and concentration, you understand that the cloud is right there in your tea, very close. You have never lost your beloved. She has just changed forms.

That is the kind of vision, the kind of insight that is needed to overcome grief. We think that we have lost him forever, but that person has not died, has not disappeared. He continues in new forms. We have to practice looking deeply to recognize his continuation and support it. "Darling, I know you are there somehow, very real to me. I am breathing for you. I am looking around for you. I enjoy life for you. And I know that you are still there very close to me and you are in me." We transform our suffering and our fear into awakened insight, and we feel much better.

When we overcome the notion of birth and death, we stop being controlled by fear. The notion of being and the notion of nonbeing can create a tremendous amount of fear. When the cloud disappears in the sky, it does not pass from being to nonbeing—it continues always. The nature of the cloud is nobirth and no-death. The nature of your beloved is like that, and you are also like that.

Appreciating Where We Are

Imagine two astronauts go to the moon, and while they're there, there's an accident and their ship can't take them back to Earth. They have only enough oxygen for two days. There is no hope of someone coming from Earth in time to rescue them. They have only two days to live.

If you were to ask them at that moment, "What is your deepest wish?" they would answer, "To be back home walking on our beautiful planet Earth." That would be enough for them; they wouldn't want anything else. They wouldn't think of being the head of a large corporation, a famous celebrity, or the president of the United States. They wouldn't want anything but to be back here—walking on Earth, enjoying every step, listening to the sounds of nature, or holding the hand of their beloved while contemplating the moon at night.

We should live every day like people who have just been rescued from dying on the moon. We are on Earth now, and we need to enjoy walking on this precious, beautiful planet. Zen Master Linji said, "The miracle is not to walk on water or fire. The miracle is to walk on the earth." I cherish that teaching. I enjoy just walking, even in busy places like airports and railway stations. Walking like that, with each step caressing our Mother Earth, we can inspire other people to do the same. We can enjoy every minute of our lives.

Finding Solid Ground

In our daily lives, our fear causes us to lose ourselves. Our body is here, but our mind is all over the place. Sometimes we plunge ourselves into a book, and the book carries us far away from our body and the reality where we are. Then, as soon as we lift our head out of the book, we're back to being carried away by worries and fear. But we rarely go back to our inner peace, to our clarity, to the Buddha nature in each of us, so that we can be in touch with Mother Earth.

Many people forget their own body. They live in an imaginary world. They have so many plans and fears, so many agitations and dreams, and they don't live in their body. While we're caught in fear and trying to plan our way out of fear, we aren't able to see all the beauty that Mother Earth offers us. Mindfulness reminds you to go to your in-breath and to be totally with your in-breath, be totally with your out-breath. Bring your mind back to your body and be in the present moment.

Look deeply straight in front of you at what is wonderful in the present moment. Mother Earth is so powerful, so generous, and so supportive. Your body is so wonderful. When you've practiced and you are solid like the earth, you face your difficulty directly and it begins to dissipate.

Practice: Breathing in the Present

Please take a moment to enjoy the simple practice of mindful breathing: "Breathing in, I know that I am breathing in; breathing out, I know that I am breathing out." If you do that with a little concentration, then you'll be able to really be there. The moment you begin to practice mindful breathing, your body and your mind begin to come back together. It takes only ten to twenty seconds to accomplish this miracle, the oneness of body and mind in the present moment. And every one of us can do it, even a child.

As the Buddha said, "The past no longer is, the future is not yet here; there is only one moment in which life is available, and that is the present moment." To meditate with mindful breathing is to bring body and mind back to the present moment so that you do not miss your appointment with life.

The Gift of Fearlessness

If you have a loved one who is facing death, she may be very afraid. If you want to be able to help your friend, you have to learn to cultivate your own nonfear. Nonfear is the basis of true happiness, and if you can offer nonfear to someone, you are giving that person the best kind of gift. If you can sit solidly with your friend during those difficult moments, you can help her die peacefully without fear. Nonfear is the cream of the Buddha's teaching.

Practicing meditation, we can generate the energies of mindfulness and concentration. These energies will lead us back to the insight that nothing is really born or dies. We can truly remove our fear of death. When we understand that we cannot be destroyed, we are liberated from fear. It is a great relief. Nonfear is the ultimate joy.

If we have fear, we can't be completely happy. If we're still running after the object of our desire, then we still have fear. Fear goes together with craving. We want to be safe and happy, so we begin to crave a particular person or object or idea (such as wealth or fame) that we think will guarantee our well-being. We can never fully satisfy our craving, so we keep running and we stay scared. If you stop running after the object of your craving—whether it's a person, a thing, or an idea—your fear will dissipate. Having no fear, you can be peaceful. With peace in your body and mind, you aren't beset by worries, and in fact you have fewer accidents. You are free.

If we can model the ability to embody nonfear and non-attachment, it is more precious than any money or material wealth. Fear spoils our lives and makes us miserable. We cling to objects and people, like a drowning person clings to any object that floats by. By practicing nonattachment and sharing this wisdom with others, we give the gift of nonfear. Everything is impermanent. This moment passes. The object of our craving walks away, but we can know happiness is always possible.

Intoxicants

We do not want our fear, our anger, our pain, so we suppress it by filling up our lives with the things provided us by modern civilization: websites, games, films, music. All these items can contain many toxins that only serve to increase our sickness, our fear.

Suppose you watch one hour of television. That seems like very little, but you know there can be a lot of violence, a lot of fear, and a lot of poisons in that one-hour program. And you practice intoxicating yourself every day. You think you're getting some kind of relief, but while entertaining yourself you continue to bring into the depths of your consciousness even more elements of pain and suffering. So the blocks of pain deep within you keep growing bigger and bigger. We intoxicate ourselves with what we consume every day. We let the television set be our children's babysitter, and our children get intoxicated every day by what they see and hear there. The Buddha terms these things *poisons*. There are poisons in us already, deep in our consciousness, and yet we open ourselves up to bring in even more poisons and toxins.

Our environment is also deeply polluted by toxins. Practicing meditation means being aware of all that is going on, not only in our body but also in the rest of the world. We are feeding ourselves and our children with poisons. That is what is happening in the present moment. If you notice this, you are awakened to the fact that we are intoxicating ourselves all day long. We have to find a way to stop consuming these intoxicants that feed our fear.

The Nature of Interbeing

When we look deeply into a sheet of paper, we see that it's full of everything in the cosmos: the sunshine, the trees, the clouds, the earth, the minerals, everything—except for one thing. It's empty of one thing only: a separate self. The sheet of paper cannot *be* by itself alone. It has to inter-be with everything else in the cosmos. That is why the word *inter-be* can be more helpful than the word *be*. In fact, to be *means* to inter-be. The sheet of paper cannot be without the sunshine, cannot be without the forest. The sheet of paper has to inter-be with the sunshine, to inter-be with the forest.

If you were to ask how the world came into existence, into being, the Buddha would say in very simple terms, "This is because that is. This is not because that is not." Because the sunshine is, the sheet of paper is. Because the tree is, the sheet of paper is. You cannot be by yourself alone. You have to inter-be with everything else in the cosmos. That is the nature of interbeing. I don't think that the word *inter-be* is in the dictionary, but I believe that it will be there soon, because it helps us to see the real nature of things, the nature of interbeing.

If you are locked into the idea of a separate self, you have great fear. But if you look deeply and are capable of seeing "you" everywhere, you lose that fear.

As a monk, I practice looking deeply every day. I don't just give lectures. I can see me in my students. I see me in my ancestors. I see my continuation everywhere in this moment. Every day I make the effort to transmit to my students the best that I have received from my teachers and from my practice.

I don't believe that I will cease to be someday. I told my friends that the twenty-first century is a hill, a beautiful hill that we will climb together as a sangha; I will be with my sangha all the way. For me that is not a problem, because I see everyone in me, and me in everyone. That is the practice of looking deeply, the practice of concentration on emptiness, the practice of interbeing.

The Story of Anathapindika

Anathapindika, who lived 2,600 years ago, was an early follower of the Buddha. Anathapindika was a businessman who was very generous, and he used his time and energy to help the destitute people of his city. He gave away a lot of his wealth to the poor, yet he did not become less wealthy. He received a lot of happiness. He had a lot of friends in his business circles, and he was loved by all of them.

Anathapindika took great pleasure in serving the Buddha. He used his wealth to buy a forested park and build a practice center called the Jeta Grove, where the Buddha and his monks could practice. The Jeta Grove became a famous practice center, and people came there to listen to the talk given by the Buddha every week.

One day the Buddha learned that his beloved disciple, Anathapindika, was very sick. He went to visit him and urged Anathapindika to practice mindful breathing while in bed. Then the Buddha asked Shariputra, a close friend of Anathapindika's, to take care of him during his illness.

Shariputra and his younger monastic brother, Ananda, went to visit Anathapindika. When they arrived, Anathapindika was so weak he could not sit up in bed to greet them. Shariputra said, "No, my friend, don't try. Just lie quietly. We will bring a few chairs to be close to you and sit together."

The first question Shariputra asked was, "Dear friend Anathapindika, how do you feel? Is the pain in your body growing worse, or has it begun to lessen?" Anathapindika said, "No, friends, the pain in me is not lessening. It is getting worse all the time."

When Shariputra heard that, he decided to offer Anathapindika a few exercises in guided meditation. As one of the most intelligent of the Buddha's disciples, Shariputra knew very well that helping Anathapindika focus his mind on the Buddha, whom he loved to serve, would give Anathapindika a lot of pleasure. Shariputra wanted to water the seeds of happiness inside Anathapindika, and he knew that talking about all the things that had made Anathapindika happy in his life would water those good seeds in him and lessen his pain in this critical time.

Shariputra invited Anathapindika to breathe in and out mindfully and to focus his attention on his happiest recollections: his work for the poor, his many acts of generosity, and the love and compassion he shared with his family and his fellow students of the Buddha.

In just five or six minutes, the pain that Anathapindika had been feeling throughout his body lessened as the seeds of happiness in him were watered, and he smiled. Watering the seeds of happiness is a very important practice for those who are sick or dying. All of us have seeds of happiness inside us, and in those difficult moments when we're sick or dying, there should be a friend sitting with us to help us touch those seeds. Otherwise seeds of fear, regret, or despair can easily sprout into big formations that overwhelm us.

When Anathapindika was able to smile, Shariputra knew that the meditation had been successful. Shariputra invited Anathapindika to continue the guided meditation. "Dear friend Anathapindika, now it is the time to practice the meditation on the six senses. Breathe in and out and practice with me."

These eyes are not me. I am not caught in these eyes.

This body is not me. I am not caught in this body.

I am life without boundaries.

The decaying of this body does not mean the end of me.

I am not limited to this body.

When someone is about to die, he may be very caught up in the idea that this body is him. He is caught in the notion that the disintegration of the body is his own disintegration. We are all very afraid of becoming nothing. But the disintegration of the body cannot affect the dying person's true nature. That's why it's very important for us to be able to look deeply to see the ways in which we are not just our bodies. Each of us is life without limit.

This body is not me. I am not caught in this body.

I am life without limit.

These eyes are not me. I am not caught in these eyes.

These ears are not me. I am not caught in these ears.

This nose is not me. I am not caught in this nose.

This tongue is not me. I am not caught in this tongue.

This body is not me. I am not caught in this body.

This mind is not me. I am not caught in this mind.

They led Anathapindika to meditate also on the objects of the six senses. The dying person may be attached to forms, sounds, body, mind, and so on, considering these things to be self; because he is losing these, he believes he is losing self. These meditations are very comforting for an ill or dying person.

These things I see are not me. I am not caught in what I see.

These sounds are not me. I am not caught in these sounds.

These smells are not me. I am not caught in these smells.

These tastes are not me. I am not caught in these tastes.

These contacts with the body are not me. I am not caught in these contacts with the body.

These thoughts are not me. I am not caught in these thoughts.

Anathapindika knew these two monks very well. Both were beloved disciples of the Buddha, and they were sitting there to support him, so he was able to do the meditation easily, even though he was gravely ill. Then Shariputra guided him in the meditation on time:

The past is not me. I am not limited by the past.

The present is not me. I am not limited by the present.

The future is not me. I am not limited by the future.

Finally they came to the meditation on being and non-being, coming and going. These are very deep teachings. Shariputra said, "Dear friend Anathapindika, everything that is arises because of causes and conditions. Everything that is has the nature not to be born and not to die, not to arrive and not to depart.

"When the body arises, it arises. It does not come from anywhere. If conditions are sufficient, the body manifests, and you perceive it as existing. When the conditions are no longer sufficient, the body is not perceived by you, and you may think of it as not existing. In fact, the nature of everything is no-birth and no-death."

Anathapindika was a very capable practitioner. When he practiced to this point, he was moved and got insight right away. He was able to touch the dimension of no-birth and no-death. He was released from the idea that he was only his body. He released the notions of birth and death, the notions of being and nonbeing, and so was able to receive and realize the gift of nonfear.

Everything that is comes to be because of a combination of causes. When the causes and conditions are sufficient, the body is present. When the causes and conditions are not sufficient, the body is absent. The same is true of eyes, ears, nose, tongue, mind; form, sound, smell, taste, touch, and so on. This may seem abstract, but it is possible for all of us to have a deep understanding of it. You have to know the true nature of dying to understand the true nature of living. If you don't understand death, you don't understand life.

The teaching of the Buddha relieves us of suffering. The basis of suffering is ignorance about the true nature of self and of the world around you. When you don't understand, you are afraid, and your fear brings you much suffering. That is why the offering of nonfear is the best kind of gift you can give, to yourself and to anyone else.

This important practice, the practice of nonfear, involves looking deeply to relieve the deep fear that is always there. If you have nonfear, your life will be happier and more beautiful, and you will be able to help many other people, just as Shariputra helped Anathapindika. The energy of nonfear is the key and the best basis for social action, for actions of compassion that protect people, protect the earth, and satisfy your needs to love and to serve.

It is entirely possible to live happily and die peacefully. We do this by seeing that we continue our manifestation in other forms. It is also possible for us to help others die peacefully, if we have the elements of solidity and nonfear in us. So many of us are afraid of nonbeing, and because of this fear, we suffer a lot. That is why the reality that we are a manifestation, and a continuation of many manifestations, should be revealed to the dying person. We are then not affected by the fear of birth and death, because we understand that birth and death are just notions. This insight can liberate us from fear.

If we know how to practice and penetrate the reality of no-birth and no-death, if we realize that coming and going are just ideas, and if our presence is solid and peaceful, we help the dying person to not be scared and not suffer much. We can help the person die peacefully. We can help ourselves live without fear and die peacefully when we understand there is no dying, only continuation. There, in the last moments of his life, Anathapindika received the greatest gift of all, nonfear— and he died beautifully, peacefully, without pain or fear.

The Power of Mindfulness

Every one of us has the capacity to be mindful, focused, understanding, and compassionate. That quality is inherent in everyone. You can call it *Buddha nature*. So when you say, "I take refuge in the Buddha," you don't mean that you take refuge in a kind of god that exists outside of you. It means that you have confidence in your capacity to understand and to love.

When the Buddha was very old, just before he died, he said, "My dear friends, my dear disciples, don't take refuge in anything outside of you. In every one of us there is a very safe island we can go to. Every time you go home to that island with mindful breathing, you create a space of relaxation, concentration, and insight. If you dwell on that island in yourself with your mindful breathing, you are safe. That is a place where you can take refuge whenever you feel fearful, uncertain, or confused."

In Plum Village we have a short poem put to music. That verse can be used to practice taking refuge.

Breathing in,
Breathing out.
Buddha is my mindfulness
Shining near and shining far.

When you practice being aware of your breathing, you generate the energy of mindfulness. This is called *mindfulness of breathing*. That energy of mindfulness is the Buddha, because a Buddha is made of mindfulness. And every one of us is capable of generating the energy of the Buddha. If you come from a Christian background, you may compare it to the Holy Spirit. The Holy Spirit can be described as the energy of God. With the practice of mindful walking and mindful breathing, you generate this powerful energy. You take refuge in that energy of mindfulness. It is a kind of light that shines forth and shows you clearly where you are and what is the next step you want to take.

When you practice mindful breathing, the energy generated helps reduce the tension in your body and your feelings. There may be tension in your body, and there may be strong emotions in you, like fear and despair. The energy of mindfulness is embracing, calming, and releasing the tension and suffering. This energy calms you and eases your fear.

Taking refuge in the island of self doesn't mean that you leave the world. It means that you go back to yourself, and you become more solid. It's possible to walk in the city and still be in the island of yourself. Your response to what's going on around you will be quite different if you are solid and not overwhelmed.

There may be tension in your body. There may be strong emotions. When you practice mindful breathing, the energy of mindfulness helps release the tension in your body and your feelings and reduce the suffering. After one or two minutes of this concrete practice of taking refuge in the safe island within yourself, you feel calm—you no longer feel trapped in fear or despair, and those feelings are transformed. I practice this verse frequently. I have been using it for nearly thirty years already, and I continue to use it.

The Buddha gave his teaching on the island of self when he was dying. He knew that many of his disciples would feel lost after he died, so he was trying to tell his disciples that they should look for the teacher within rather than relying on the teacher outside—that the body of the teacher may disintegrate, but the teaching has already entered the student. If you go back to the island of yourself, you will see the teacher in you.

There's no real difference between inside and outside. In fact, when we're inside we can be more in touch with the outside. If you're not there inside, if you're not yourself, there's no real contact with the world outside. The way out is in. If you get deeply in touch with the inside, you get in touch with the outside too; and if you're able to get deeply in touch with the outside, you can get in touch with the inside at the same time.

Going back to your island generates mindfulness and concentration. Whenever you are caught by an emotion like fear, anger, or despair, you go back to the island within yourself and practice this gatha to take refuge. I'm sure that you will feel much better after some minutes of this practice. When you find yourself in a dangerous or scary situation, when you are very sick, anytime you don't know exactly what to do, this is what you should practice. If everyone practiced this, there would be enough calm, peace, and clarity for us to get ourselves out of every difficult situation. The practice of taking refuge can bring us joy and peace in our daily lives.

Cultivating the Energy of Mindfulness

Mindfulness is a kind of energy that can help bring our minds back to our bodies so that we can be established well in the here and now, so that we can get deeply in touch with life and its many wonders and truly live our lives. Mindfulness allows us to be aware of what is going on in the present moment—in our bodies, in our feelings, in our perceptions, in the world.

We know that the morning is beautiful—the hills, the mist, the sunrise. We want to get in touch with that beauty and allow it into our hearts. We know this is very nourishing. But sometimes an emotion or feeling comes up that prevents us from enjoying what's happening in the here and now. While another person is able to let the mountains, the glorious sunrise, the beauty of nature penetrate fully into his body and mind, we are blocked by our worries, our fear, and our anger, and the beauty of the sunrise cannot really enter us. Our emotions prevent us from getting in touch with the wonders of life, the kingdom of God, the Pure Land of the Buddha.

What should we do in these circumstances? We think we have to remove that feeling or emotion to be free again, so the beautiful sunrise can penetrate us. We consider our fear, anger, and worries as enemies. We think that without them we would be free, and that these feelings get in the way so we cannot receive the nourishment we need.

It is in moments like this that we stick to our mindful breathing and gently recognize our afflictions, whether anger, frustration, or fear. Suppose we are feeling worry or anxiety. We practice, "Breathing in, I know that anxiety is in me. Breathing out, I smile to my anxiety." Maybe you have a habit of worrying. Even if you know it's neither necessary nor useful, you still worry. You'd like to ban worry and get rid of it, because you know that when you worry you can't get in touch with the wonders of life and you can't be happy. So you get angry at your worry; you don't want it. But worry is a part of you, and that's why when your worry comes up, you have to know how to handle it tenderly and peacefully. You can do it if you have the energy of mindfulness. You cultivate the energy of mindfulness with mindful breathing and mindful walking, and with that energy, you can recognize and tenderly embrace your worry, fear, and anger.

When your baby suffers and cries, you don't want to punish him or her, because your baby is you. Your fear and anger are like your baby. Don't imagine that you can just throw them out the window. Don't be violent toward your anger, your fear, and your worries. The practice is simply to recognize them. Continue to practice mindful breathing and mindful walking; then, with the energy generated by your practice, you can recognize intense feelings, smile to them, and embrace them tenderly. This is the practice of nonviolence with your worries, fear, and anger. If you get angry with your anger, it is multiplied ten times. This is not wise. You already suffer a lot, and if you get angry with your anger, you will suffer more. A baby may not be pleasant when she cries and kicks, but her mother picks her up tenderly and holds her in her arms, and the mother's tenderness penetrates the baby. After a few minutes, the baby feels better and may stop crying.

It's the energy of mindfulness that empowers you to recognize your pain and sorrow and embrace them tenderly. You feel some relief, and your baby is quiet. Now you can enjoy the beautiful sunrise and allow yourself to be nourished by the wonders of life around you as well as inside you.

Taking Mindfulness with Us

Like many of us, you may be in the habit of carrying your cell phone around with you everywhere you go. You think you can't live without your cell phone. You are fearful when you forget and leave your phone at home. You worry when your battery starts to run low.

When we practice mindfulness, we can take our practice with us wherever we go, just like you take your phone with you; but mindfulness doesn't take up any space or make your bags any heavier, and your batteries never run down. Whenever you go somewhere, your practice goes with you.

Our daily lives need to have a spiritual dimension to help us develop our capacity for taking good care of our pain and fear as well as our happiness. If we practice mindfulness, we always have a place to be when we are afraid. If we nourish and cultivate our mindfulness practice, it will become vigorous and robust. Everywhere we go, we will have our practice, so we will have confidence—more confidence than our cell phones can bring us. We can stand firm through any difficulty.

Everyone has the seed of mindfulness inside. Everyone is capable of breathing in mindfully, even very young people. Everyone can drink their tea mindfully; everyone can take a step in mindfulness. When you're inhabited by the energy of mindfulness, you speak, eat, and walk in mindfulness. The energy of mindfulness is alive in you.

Mindfulness carries within it the energy of concentration, so the seed of concentration is also in you. There are practices of concentration that can liberate us from fear, anger, and despair. Generating the energies of mindfulness and concentration in your daily life, you learn to transform your fear and anger and let go of suffering. And then along with mindfulness and concentration comes insight. Insight is wisdom, understanding. The seed of wisdom, of perfect understanding, is in each of us. Awareness is mindfulness, concentration, and insight.

When I see you walking in mindfulness, with solidity, with happiness, I see the holiness in you. We might even call you "your holiness." It's true. Every one of us has our holiness, because we have the Buddha inside of us. When the Buddha is alive inside us, we don't suffer, and happiness is possible.

Learning to Stop

The practice of meditation offered by the Buddha has two parts: stopping and looking deeply. The first part of meditation is stopping. If you're like most of us, since you were born, you've been running. Now it's a strong habit that many generations of your ancestors also had before you and transmitted to you—the habit of running, being tense, and being carried away by many things, so that your mind is not totally, deeply, peacefully in the present moment. You get accustomed to looking at things in a very superficial way and being carried away by wrong perceptions and the negative emotions that result. This leads to behaving wrongly and making life miserable.

The practice is to train yourself to *stop*—stop running after all these things. Even if you don't have irritation, anger, fear, or despair, you're still running with this or that project, or this or that line of thinking, and you're not at peace. So even (or especially) at those times when you have no problem at all, train yourself to be here, to be relaxed, to stop, to come back to the wonders of the present moment.

When your mind is still, you see things deeply. If you really practice stopping, then you don't need to practice looking deeply, because you'll be seeing things very deeply already. Stopping and looking deeply are one; they're two aspects of the same reality. If you're focused on something important, that forces your mind to be concentrated, and when you are concentrated, you're stopping and looking deeply.

So stopping and being in touch with what is positive, you are fresh, you are clear, you are smiling. You are being fed with the nourishment of the practice, and you are able to nourish others with your clarity of mind, your smile, your joy.

Even amid the wonders of the present moment, it may be that you have a number of difficulties; but if you look deeply, you'll see you still have maybe eighty percent positive things to be in touch with and enjoy. So don't run. Come back to the present moment. By doing so, you cultivate concentration, and you'll see things more deeply and clearly. That training is very simple but so important.

Dwell peacefully in your in-breath and out-breath in the present moment. When the emotion is too strong and the breathing isn't enough to get you to stop and relax, go out and walk. Focus on your footsteps to help your mind stop. Don't let your mind carry you away with thinking, judgments, ir-ritation, strong feelings, or projects. Come back to the present moment, stop, and relax. Stop, and release the agitation and tension in you. Even if you're not experiencing strong emo-tions, train yourself so that when you do need to think about something, contemplate something, look deeply into something, you'll be able to sit quietly and look deeply and make your plan.

With practice, you can release the tension and reduce the pain in your body, and you can recognize painful feelings inside, know how to embrace them, and release the tension in your feelings, bringing relief. You can create a feeling of joy and happiness whenever you want.

With good practice, you will no longer be afraid of obstacles and difficulties. You will know how to cope with the difficulties that arise. With practice that is solid, there is no reason to be fearful anymore, because you have seen the path. When you know how to handle your body, your feelings, your perceptions, there is no need to worry anymore.

Whether standing, walking, or sitting in meditation, you can use your in-breath and out-breath to help yourself to stop. You stop totally in the present moment. And when you stop, you are master of your body and your mind. You will not allow your habit energy to carry you away in compulsively thinking of something in the past or the future, of this or that project. You train yourself to stop, to relax and be at peace. Sitting meditation is not for fighting. You let go of everything.

When a thought comes, you say hello, and then you say good-bye right away. When other thoughts come, just say hello and say good-bye again. Don't fight. Don't say, "Oh, I'm so bad, I think of so many things!" You don't need to think like that. You just say hi and bye, relax and let go. You bring your mind to the present moment and rest in awareness of your body. It's like soaking mung beans in water. You don't need to force the water to enter the mung bean. You let the mung bean *be* in the water, and slowly, slowly it goes in. Gradually the mung bean gets saturated, swollen and tender. The same is true for you. Letting go, the tension will be released slowly, slowly, slowly. And you will become more relaxed and more peaceful. The training is to just keep bringing your mind back to the present moment with your body.

When you walk, usually your body is here but your mind is somewhere else. Here again, the training is to come back to the present moment. Your body and your mind are unified. It's very profound. And you see things in a clearer way, a more peaceful way. If some negative thinking comes, just say hello and be aware of that judgment. It could have come from your father, your mother, or somebody else who influenced you. So let go and smile to it. This is your mindful body—meaning, your body has your mind in it. We train ourselves to always have a mindful body, so that when you sit, you know that you are sitting, and your mind is fully in your sitting body. When you walk, your mind is fully in your walking body. You know each time you put your foot on the ground, peacefully, lovingly, deeply.

Meditation as Nourishment

Meditation can bring you happiness right away. You stop letting your worries, your anxieties, your projects carry you away. You come back to the present moment, you touch what is still positive in you, and you have the joy of meditation, the joy of the practice according to the teaching of the Buddha. The joy of meditation is like your food, your daily food. If you don't have that daily food, that joy, you're like a withered flower. When you get back in touch with the awareness that there are plenty of positive conditions still present, your mind becomes very joyful and you smile to yourself; you look fresh and alive. So don't deprive yourself of that food, the joy of meditation.

Body and Mind Are One

When you let go mentally, you relax physically, because the body and the mind are two aspects of one reality. When your mind is too tense, when your mind has too many difficulties, it affects your body day after day. Of course your body has to have some movement and circulation too, so that tension doesn't build up.

Through stopping, whether in walking or sitting meditation, you are in control of the situation. You are the sovereign of your body and your mind. Don't allow that agitation, fear, or anxiety to carry you away. When you are carried away by anxiety and fear, you are like a queen or king deposed. The practice here is to regain your sovereignty. When you walk mindfully, when you sit mindfully, you regain sovereignty over yourself.

When your mind is in the present moment, you can see deeply what brings you suffering and what brings you happiness. Your concentration and insight will allow you to think, act, and speak with more clarity.

We know that other people are impermanent, but in daily life we assume that they are permanent. With this awareness, we can treat others with more love and understanding. They will soon be gone. With this awareness, we can also have more understanding of our own role in our suffering. Instead of blaming others, we can look at our own being and work on whatever unskillfulness on our part may have contributed to our difficulty with another.

Calm in the Storm

Every time we feel a strong wave of fear, anger, or jealousy, we can do something to care for this negative energy so it does not destroy us. There doesn't need to be any conflict between one element and another element of our being. There should only be an effort of taking care and being able to transform. We need to have a nonviolent attitude toward our suffering, our pain, our fear.

When we have a strong emotion like fear or despair, it can be overwhelming. But with practice, we know we can learn how to embrace our fear, because we know that in each one of us there is the seed of mindfulness. If we practice touching that seed every day while walking, sitting, breathing, smiling, or eating, we cultivate that energy of mindfulness. And then anytime we need that energy, we just touch that seed, and right away the energy of mindfulness will come up and we can use it to embrace our emotions. If we succeed just once in doing so, we will have a little more peace and will be less afraid of that strong emotion the next time it comes up.

Fear Pays a Visit

Suppose you have a lot of pain, sorrow, or fear down deep in your consciousness. Many of us have big blocks of pain and suffering in the depths of our consciousness that we cannot bear to look at. We have to keep ourselves very busy to ensure that these unwelcome guests do not come and pay us a visit. We busy ourselves with other "guests"—we pick up a magazine or a book to read, we turn on the television, or we play music. We do anything and everything we can to fill our attention with something. That is the practice of repressing.

Most of us adopt this embargo response. We do not want to open the door for our fear, our sorrow, and our depression to come up, so we bring in all manner of other things to occupy us. And there are always plenty of things available to help us distract ourselves from what's happening inside. There are many ways we can entertain ourselves—especially watching television. Television can be used as a kind of drug. When the suffering in us is too much to bear, we sometimes turn on the television set to forget our pain. It fills our living room with images and sounds. Even if what we're watching isn't satisfying, we often don't have the courage to turn off the TV. Why? Because although it's uninteresting or even disturbing, we think it's better than going home to ourselves and touching the pain within. Distraction is the policy for many of us. Some of us choose to live in a television-free zone, like we have nonsmoking zones or nondrinking zones. But many others of us practice television watching or video game playing to cover up our discomfort.

I know one family that watched television shows every night. One day they went to the flea market and saw a Buddha statue. They bought it for the house, but since their house was small, there was no place to put the statue. So they decided to put it on top of the television set, as it was a clean and presentable spot. I happened to visit them just after they had installed the Buddha. And I said, "Dear friends, the statue and the television don't belong together because these two things are poles apart. The Buddha is for us to go home to ourselves, and the television is to help us run away from ourselves."

Belly Breathing

There are several simple methods for taking care of our strong emotions. One is "belly breathing," breathing from the abdomen. When we are caught in a strong emotion like fear or anger, our practice is to bring our attention down to the abdomen. To stay on the level of the intellect is not safe. Strong emotions are like a storm, and to stand in the middle of a storm is very dangerous. Yet that's what most of us do when we get upset; we stay out in the storm of our feelings, and they overwhelm us. Instead, we have to ground ourselves by bringing our attention downward. We focus on our abdomen and practice mindful breathing, just giving all of our attention to the rise and fall of the belly.

Making It Through the Storm

When you look at a tree during a storm, you see that its branches and leaves are swaying back and forth violently in the strong wind. You have the impression that the tree will not be able to withstand the storm. You are like that when you're gripped by a strong emotion. Like the tree, you feel vulnerable. You can break at any time. But if you direct your attention down to the trunk of the tree, you see things differently. You see that the tree is solid and deeply rooted in the ground. If you focus your attention on the trunk of the tree, you realize that because the tree is firmly rooted in the soil, it cannot be blown away.

Each of us, in a sitting or standing position, is like the tree. When the storm of your emotion is passing by, you should not stay in the thick of the storm, the level of the brain or the chest. When you are overwhelmed by strong emotions, don't stay there—it's too dangerous. Bring your focus down to your navel—that is the trunk, the most solid part of yourself—and practice mindful breathing. Become aware of the rise and fall of your abdomen. Doing this in a stable position, such as the sitting position, you feel much better. Just breathe. Don't think of anything. Breathe through the movement, the rise and fall, of your abdomen. Practice in this way for ten or fifteen minutes, and the strong emotion will pass on through.

Emotions Are Only Emotions

Meditation has two aspects: stopping and calming is the first, and looking deeply to transform is the second. When you have enough energy of mindfulness, you can look deeply into any emotion and discover the true nature of that emotion. If you can do that, you will be able to transform the emotion.

Of course, emotions have deep roots in us. They are so strong, we think we will not survive them if we let them be. We deny and suppress them until finally they explode and cause hurt to ourselves and others. But an emotion is just an emotion. It comes, it stays for a while, and then it goes away. Why should we hurt ourselves or others just because of one emotion? We are so much more than our emotions.

If we know how to practice looking deeply, we will be able to identify and uproot the sources of our painful emotions. Just practicing embracing the emotions can already be very helpful. If, during the critical moment when the emotion is there, we know how and where to take refuge, if we are able to breathe in and out and focus our attention on the rise and fall of our abdomen for fifteen or twenty or even twenty-five minutes, then the storm will roll away, and we will be aware that we can survive. When we succeed in surviving strong emotions, we experience a more solid peace of mind. Once we have got the practice, we are no longer afraid. The next time a strong emotion arises, it becomes easier. We already know that we can survive it.

If we can relax when our strong emotions come, then we don't pass fear on to our children and to future generations. If we stay with our fear, suppressing it and then letting it explode, we are sharing that fear with the young people around us, and they will consume it and pass it on. But if we know how to handle our own fear, we will be more able to help our loved ones and our young ones handle theirs. We can be with them and say, "Darling, breathe in and out with me. Pay attention to the rise and fall of your belly." Because they have seen you do this, they will be more likely to listen to you. Because you are there and you offer your energy of mindfulness and your solidity, your child or your partner will be able to cross the white water of emotion. She will know that with her loved one at her side, she, like you, can survive the strong emotion. Modeling calm in the face of fear, and teaching young people how to weather their own storms, you are teaching a very valuable skill that might even save their lives in the future.

Transforming the Fear Around Us

Many of us spend a lot of our time acting out of fear of the past or the present, and in doing that, we affect each other and the larger society. We create a culture of fear. When fear comes up and we're upset and worried, the first thing we need to do is acknowledge that fear. We can recognize and embrace it rather than acting it out. All around us people are afraid and acting out of fear. In the midst of all this fear, we all long for peace and security.

Sometimes it's tempting to ridicule the fear of others because it reminds us of our own fear. We have been taught to keep our fear out of sight and unacknowledged. How can we let go of fear and relinquish the anger and violence that it animates in us? We have to listen deeply and learn to practice the way the Buddha practiced to let go of his own fear and violence. Practicing mindfulness of fear and looking deeply into its origin provide the answer.

Fear of Terrorism

Nowadays, when we fly on an airplane, everybody is suspect. We fear that anyone could be a terrorist. Anyone could be carrying explosive chemicals or wearing a bomb. We all have to go through a body scan. Everyone is fearful of everyone and everything else. Even if you wear a monk's robe like I do, you have to get scanned or searched, because the fear is so prevalent. The people who came before us created this climate of fear, and now it has grown and grown. We don't know how to handle our suffering. Few people know how to let go of fearfulness.

We develop a wish for vengeance; we want to punish those who made us suffer, and we think doing so will make us suffer less. We want to do violence to them, to punish them. When a terrorist brings explosives onto a bus or a plane, everyone dies. The terrorist's wish to punish is born from his suffering. He doesn't know how to handle his own suffering, and he looks to relieve it by punishing others.

The Buddha said, "I have looked deeply into the state of mind of unhappy people and have seen hidden under their suffering a very sharp knife. Because they don't see that sharp knife in themselves, it is difficult for them to deal with suffering."

Your fear is buried deep in your heart, a sharp knife covered over by many layers. That sharp knife is what makes you behave in such an unkind way. You do not see the knife or the arrow in your heart, but it causes you to make other people suffer. You can learn to recognize that knife inside. And once you've found it, if you can remove the knife in your own heart, then you can help find and remove the knife in the heart of another. The pain caused by that sharp knife has been there for a long time. As long as you continue to hold onto it, your pain magnifies and grows so large that you want to punish those you think are the cause of your suffering.

A Revolution of Compassion

We all have original fear in us, but it is not just we, as individuals, who are afraid. Many countries and regions of the world are burning with fear, suffering, and hatred. If only to ease our own suffering, we have to return to ourselves and seek to understand why we are caught up in so much violence and fear. What has caused terrorists to hate so much that they are willing to sacrifice their own lives and create so much suffering for other people? We see their great hatred, but what is driving it? Perceived injustice. Of course we have to find a way to stop the violence. We may even need to keep people separated while they are still a danger to others. But we also need to ask, "What responsibility do we have for the injustice in the world?"

We do not like feeling afraid. Often, if we hold on to our fear, it turns into anger. We are angry that we are afraid. We are angry at whatever or whomever we perceive as causing our fear and keeping us afraid. Some people spend their whole lives trying only to take revenge on whatever or whomever they think caused their suffering. This kind of motivation can only bring suffering, not only to others but also to the one who feels it.

Hatred, anger, and fear are like burning fires that can be put out by compassion. But where do we find compassion? It isn't sold in the supermarket; if it were, we would only need to bring it home and we could dissolve all the hatred and violence in the world very easily. But compassion can only be produced in our own heart, by our own practice.

Sometimes someone we love—our child, our spouse, or our parent—says or does something cruel, and we feel hurt. We think it is only we who suffer. But the other person is suffering as well. If he weren't suffering, he wouldn't have spoken or acted in a way that hurt us. The person we love hasn't seen a way to transform his suffering, so he just pours out all his fear and anger on us. Our responsibility is to produce the energy of compassion that first calms down our own heart and then allows us to help the other person. If we punish the other person, he will just suffer more, and the cycle will continue.

Responding to violence with violence can only bring more violence, more injustice, and more suffering—not only to the ones we seek to punish but also to ourselves. This wisdom is in every one of us. When we breathe deeply, we can touch this seed of wisdom in us. I know that if the energy of wisdom and compassion in all people could be nourished for even one week, it would reduce the level of fear, anger, and hatred in the world. I urge all of us to practice calming and concentrating our minds, watering the seeds of wisdom and compassion that are already there in us, and learning the art of mindful consumption. If we can do this, we will create a true peaceful revolution, the only kind of revolution that can help us out of this difficult situation.

Seeds of Terrorism

"Terrorists" are everywhere. They're not only the people who blow up buses and markets. When we are angry, when we behave in a very angry, violent way, then we are not so different from the terrorists we demonize, because we have that same knife of anger in our hearts. When we're not mindful in our words, we say things that can hurt others and cause a lot of pain. That is a kind of intimidation, a kind of terrorism. Many people use hurtful words against children. That knife of hurt may twist in a child's heart every day for the rest of his life. In our family, in our society, on our planet, every day we create more people with knives in their hearts. And because they hold knives in their hearts, their suffering and rage overwhelm their families, their society, the world.

Compassionate Listening

Much of our suffering comes from wrong perceptions. To remove that hurt, we have to remove our wrong perception. "I see him or her as doing this or that. But maybe the reality is not exactly like that. There are a number of hidden points I didn't know. I need to listen to him or her more, in order to understand better." The people who we think have created our suffering likewise may have wrong perceptions about us. When you make the effort to listen and hear the other side of the story, your understanding increases and your hurt diminishes.

The first thing we can do in these situations is to acknowledge internally that the pictures we have in our head, what we think happened, may not be accurate. Our practice is to breathe and walk until we are more calm and relaxed.

The second thing we can do, when we are ready, is to tell the people who we think have hurt us that we are suffering and that we know our suffering may have come from our own wrong perception. Instead of coming to the other person or people with an accusation, we can come to them for help and ask them to explain, to help us understand why they have said or done those things.

There is a third thing we need to do, if we can. The third thing is very hard, perhaps the hardest. We need to listen very carefully to the other person's response to truly understand and try to correct our perception. With this, we may find that we have been the victim of our wrong perceptions. Most likely the other person has also been a victim of wrong perceptions.

Deep listening and loving speech are very powerful practices. With them, we can create good communication and find out what is really going on. If we are sincere in wanting to learn the truth, and if we know how to use gentle speech and deep listening, we are much more likely to be able to hear others' honest perceptions and feelings. In that process, we may discover that they too have wrong perceptions. After listening to them fully, we have an opportunity to help them correct their wrong perceptions. If we approach our hurts this way, we have the chance to turn our fear and anger into opportunities for deeper, more honest relationships.

The Heart Is a Bridge

When you take out the knife of anger and mistrust that is pointed to your heart, your heart becomes a bridge. If you can undo attachment, craving, and fear, you start to see the other shore, the shore of liberation. We have to act with loving kindness, because when hatred and anger are running rampant, we cannot resolve anything. We cannot remove violence with hatred and anger. We can only remove violence and fear with compassion and love.

First you say, "Dear friend, I have a sharp knife in my heart. I want to take it out."

If the other person takes you up on your offer to listen and begins to share, be prepared to practice deep, compassionate listening. Listen with all your mindfulness and concentration. Your sole desire is to give him or her a chance to speak out. Compassionate, deep listening means that the other person, or the other nation, has a chance to say what they have never had the chance or the courage to say, because no one ever listened deeply to them before.

At first, their speech may be full of condemnation, bitterness, and blame. Do your best to continue sitting there calmly and listening. To listen in this way is to give them a chance to heal their suffering and misperceptions. If you interrupt, deny, or correct what they say, you will cut off the process of restoring communication, of reconciliation. Deep listening allows the other person to speak even if what he says contains misperceptions and injustice. When listening deeply to the other person, not only do you recognize his wrong perceptions but you also realize that you too have wrong perceptions about yourself and the other person. Later, when both of you are calm and the other person feels more trust and confidence in you, you can slowly and skillfully begin to correct their wrong perceptions. Using loving speech, you can point out how they have misunderstood you or the situation. Using loving speech, you can also help the other person understand your difficulties. You can help each other release those wrong perceptions, which are the cause of all anger, hatred, and violence.

Restoring Communication

The intention of deep listening and loving speech is to restore communication, because once communication is restored, everything is possible, including peace and reconciliation. I have seen many couples successfully practice deep listening and loving speech to heal difficult or broken relationships. Many fathers and sons, mothers and daughters, and husbands and wives have brought peace and happiness back to their families through this practice. With the practice of deep, compassionate listening and loving speech, they have reconciled. Leaders of countries can also reconcile using compassionate listening and loving speech.

We are all capable of recognizing that we're not the only ones who suffer when there is a hard situation. The other person in that situation suffers as well, and we are partly responsible for his or her suffering. When we realize this, we can look at the other person with the eyes of compassion and let understanding bloom. With the arrival of understanding, the situation changes and communication is possible.

Any real peace process has to begin within ourselves, within our own group and our own people. We should not continue to blame the other side for not practicing peace. We have to practice peace to help the other side make peace.

Blue Sky Above
the Clouds

In our society, there is so much fear, suffering, violence, despair, and confusion. But there is also, at the same time, the beautiful blue sky. Sometimes the blue of the sky reveals itself to us entirely. Sometimes it reveals half of itself, sometimes just a little bit of blue peeks through, and sometimes none at all. Storms, clouds, and fog hide the blue sky. The kingdom of heaven can be hidden by a cloud of ignorance or by a tempest of anger, violence, and fear. But if we practice mindfulness, it's possible to be aware that even if the weather is very foggy, cloudy, or stormy, the blue sky is always there for us above the clouds. Remembering this keeps us from sinking into despair.

While preaching in the wilderness of Judea, John the Baptist urged people to repent because "the kingdom of God is at hand." I understand *to repent* as *to stop*. He wanted us to stop engaging in acts of violence, craving, and hatred. To repent means to wake up and be aware that our fear, anger, and craving are covering up the blue sky.

To repent means to begin anew. We admit our transgressions, and we bathe ourselves in the clear waters of the spiritual teaching to love our neighbors as ourselves. We commit to letting go of our resentment, hatred, and pride. We start over with a fresh mind, a fresh heart determined to do better. After being baptized by John, Jesus taught the same thing. This teaching goes perfectly with the teaching of Buddhism.

If we know how to transform our despair, violence, and fear, the vast blue sky will reveal itself to us and to those around us. Everything we are looking for can be found in the present moment, including the Pure Land, the kingdom of God, and our Buddha nature. It is possible for us to touch the kingdom of God right here with our eyes, our feet, our arms, and our mind. When you are concentrated, when your mind and body become one, you need only make one step and there you are in the kingdom of heaven. When you are mindful, when you are free, anything you touch, whether it is oak leaves or snow, is in the kingdom of heaven. Everything you hear, the sound of the birds or the whistling wind, all belong to the kingdom of heaven.

The basic condition for touching the kingdom of God is freedom from fear, despair, anger, and craving. Mindfulness practice allows us to recognize the presence of the cloud, the fog, and the storms. But it also helps us recognize the blue sky behind it all. We have enough intelligence, courage, and stability to help the blue sky reveal itself again.

People ask me, "What can I do to help the kingdom of heaven reveal itself?" This is a very practical question. It is the same as asking, "What can I do to reduce the violence and fear that are overwhelming my community and our society?" This is something that many of us have asked.

When you take a step with stability, solidity, and freedom, you help clear the sky of despair. When hundreds of people walk mindfully together, producing the energy of solidity, stability, freedom, and joy, we help our society. When we know how to look at another person with compassionate eyes, when we know how to smile at him with the spirit of understanding, we are helping the kingdom of heaven reveal itself. When we breathe in and out mindfully, we help the Pure Land reveal itself. In our daily lives, every single moment we can do something to help the kingdom of God reveal itself. Don't allow yourself to be overwhelmed by despair. You can make good use of every minute and every hour of your daily life.

When we act as a community of practitioners, infused with the energy of mindfulness and compassion, we are powerful. When we are part of a spiritual community, we have a lot of joy and can better resist the temptation to be overwhelmed by despair. Despair is a great temptation in our century. Alone, we are vulnerable and afraid. If we try to go to the ocean as a single drop of water, we will evaporate before we ever arrive. But if we go as a river, if we go as a community, we are sure to arrive at the ocean. With a community to walk with us, support us, and always remind us of the blue sky, we'll never lose our faith, and our fear dissolves. Whether we are political or business leaders, social workers, teachers, or parents, we can all use a reminder that the blue sky is still there with us. We all need a community, a sangha, to prevent us from sinking in the swamp of despair.

The Community Is Our Body

Community building is the most important action of our century. As individuals, we have suffered tremendously. Due to the predominance of individualism, families are breaking down, and society has become deeply divided. For the twenty-first century to be a time of spirituality, the spirit of togetherness must guide us. We should learn to do things together, to share our ideas and the deep aspiration in our hearts. We have to learn to see the sangha, our community of spiritual support, as our own body. We need each other in order to practice solidity, freedom, and compassion so that we can remind each other that there's always hope.

When we have a community to practice mindfulness with, we can sit in meditation together, and it's very powerful. In life, people produce food, objects, and technology, among many other things. In a sangha, we also produce things. We produce the powerful energy of peace, the powerful energy of mindfulness. People can go to the supermarket to buy food or lightbulbs. But to produce mindful energy, we need to be with our community, our sangha, and produce this energy through our sitting, walking, and peaceful and joyful living.

This takes practice and training. I invite you to think deeply about practicing mindfulness as a wonderful way of providing spiritual food for yourself and your community. You can nourish the world with that energy. When you see that this practice provides nourishment for the world, then you will feel very joyful, because you are connected with all of life in a real way, and you are serving life.

Communication Keeps Us Safe

If we want safety, we have to build it. What do we build safety with? Fortresses, bombs, or airplanes are not going to take away our fear; in fact, they will more likely increase it. The United States of America has a very powerful military and the most advanced weapons in the world, but the American people don't feel safe. They feel very afraid and vulnerable. So there must be something else—a way to take genuine refuge, so that we can really feel safe. We have to learn to build safety with our in-breath and our out-breath. We have to learn to build safety with our steps, with our way of acting and reacting, with our words and our efforts to build communication.

You can't feel safe if you're not in good communication with the people you live with or see regularly. You can't feel safe if those around you don't look at you with friendliness and compassion. In the way you speak, sit, and walk, you can show the other person that she is safe in your presence, because you are coming to her in peace. In this way, you generate confidence. Your peace and compassion help the other person feel safe. This allows her to relate to you with compassion and understanding, and you too will feel safer. Safety is not an individual matter. Helping the other person feel safe is the best guarantee for your safety.

Your country won't be safe if you don't do anything to help other countries feel safe with you. If the United States wants safety, it has to take care of the safety of other nations also. If Great Britain wants safety, it has to think of the safety of other groups of people. Any of us could be victims of violence and terrorism. No country is immune. It's so clear that police, armed forces, and even massive firepower can't guarantee us real safety. Maybe the first thing we have to do is to say, "Dear friend, I am aware that you want to live in safety. I too want to live in safety, so why don't we work together?" This is a very simple thing for us to do—yet we don't do it.

Communication is the practice. We live in a time when there are so many sophisticated means for communication— e-mail, cell phones, text, Twitter, Facebook—yet it is very difficult for individuals, groups, and nations to communicate with each other. We can't seem to use our words to speak, so we end up using bombs instead. When we arrive at the point where we can't communicate with our words and we have to use guns, we have succumbed to despair.

We have to learn how to communicate. If we can show a group we are in conflict with that they have nothing to be afraid of, then we can begin to trust each other. In Asian countries, people often greet each other by bowing and joining their palms to form a lotus flower. In the West, when people meet, they shake hands. I learned that this tradition comes from medieval times, when people were afraid of each other. Every time they met, they wanted to show that they weren't carrying any weapons.

Now we have to do the same thing. With our actions, we can say, "Dear friend, I have no weapons. See? Touch for yourself. I am not harmful." This is the kind of practice that can build trust. With trust and communication, dialogue becomes possible.

Since the so-called war on terror began, we have spent billions of dollars but have only created more violence, hate, and fear. We have not succeeded in removing fear, hatred, and resentment, either in their outward expressions such as terrorism or, most importantly, in the minds of the people. It's time to contemplate and find a better way to bring peace to ourselves and the world. Only with the practice of deep listening and gentle communication can we help remove wrong perceptions that are at the foundation of fear, hatred, and violence. You cannot remove wrong perceptions with a gun.

Transforming Fear into Love

The Four Mantras

We have a great, habitual fear inside ourselves. We're afraid of many things—of our own death, of losing our loved ones, of change, of being alone. The practice of mindfulness helps us to touch nonfear. It's only here and now that we can experience total relief, total happiness.

Sorrow, fear, and depression are like a kind of garbage. But these bits of garbage are part of real life, and we must look deeply into their nature. We can practice so as to turn these bits of garbage into flowers. We should not throw anything out. All we have to do is learn the art of composting, of transforming our garbage into flowers. In the practice of Buddhism, we see that all mental formations—including compassion, love, fear, sorrow, and despair—are organic in nature. We don't need to be afraid of any of them, because transformation is always possible. With just a smile and mindful breathing, we can start to transform them. When we feel fear or irritation or depression, we can recognize their presence and practice the mantras below.

A mantra is a kind of magic formula that, once uttered, can entirely change a situation. It can change us, and it can change others. But this magic formula must be spoken in concentration, with body and mind focused as one. What you say in this state of being becomes a mantra. I share these four mantras as supports for the practice of coming back to really be there for ourselves and our loved ones, releasing fear, cultivating true love, and restoring communication. These mantras can be very effective for watering the seeds of happiness in yourself and your beloved and for transforming fear, suffering, and loneliness.

Mantra for Offering Your Presence

The most precious gift you can give to the one you love is your true presence. So the first mantra is very simple: "Dear one, I am here for you."

In our everyday life, most of us have very little time to cultivate our love. We are all so busy. In the morning while eating breakfast, we don't take time to look at the people we love. We eat very quickly while thinking about other things, and sometimes we even hold a newspaper that blocks out the faces of our loved ones. In the evening when we come home, we are too tired to be able to look at them.

When you love someone, the best thing you can offer that person is your presence. How can you love if you are not there? Come back to yourself, look into his eyes, and say, "Darling, you know something? I'm here for you." You're offering him your presence. You're not preoccupied with the past or the future; you are there for your beloved. You must say this with your body and with your mind at the same time, and then you will see the transformation.

Mantra for Recognizing Your Beloved

The second mantra is, "Darling, I know you are there, and I am so happy."

To be there is the first step, and recognizing the presence of the other person is the second step. Because you are fully there, you recognize that the presence of your beloved is something very precious. You embrace your beloved with mindfulness, and he or she will bloom like a flower. To be loved means first of all to be recognized as existing.

These first two mantras can bring happiness right away, even if your beloved is not there in your physical presence. You can use the telephone or e-mail to say them. "Dear one, I know that you are there, and it makes me very happy." This is real meditation. In this particular meditation, there is love, compassion, joy, and freedom—the four elements of true love as described by the Buddha.

Mantra for Relieving Suffering

The third mantra is what you practice when your beloved is suffering: "Darling, I know you're suffering. That's why I am here for you."

Even before you do anything to help, your wholehearted presence already brings some relief, because when we suffer, we have great need for the presence of the person we love. If we are suffering and the person we love ignores us, we suffer more. So what you can do—right away—is to manifest your true presence to your beloved and say the mantra with all your mindfulness: "Dear one, I know that you are suffering. That is why I am here for you." And already your loved one will feel better.

Your presence is a miracle, your understanding of his or her pain is a miracle, and you are able to offer this aspect of your love immediately. Really try to be there, for yourself, for life, for the people you love. Recognize the presence of those who live in the same place as you, and try to be there when one of them is suffering, because your presence is so precious for this person.

Mantra for Reaching Out to Ask for Help

The fourth mantra is a little bit more difficult: "Dear one, I am suffering; please help."

This mantra is for when you are suffering and you believe that your beloved has caused your suffering. If someone else had done the same wrong to you, you would have suffered less. But this is the person you love the most, so you suffer deeply, and the last thing you feel like doing is to ask that person for help. You prefer to go to your room, lock the door, and cry there all alone. So now it is your pride that is the obstacle to reconciliation and healing. According to the teaching of the Buddha, in true love there is no place for pride.

When you are suffering like this, you must go to the person you love and ask for his or her help. That is true love. Do not let pride keep you apart. You must overcome your pride. You must always go to him or her. That is what this mantra is for. Practice for yourself first, to bring about oneness of your body and mind before going to the other person to say the fourth mantra: "Dear one, I am suffering; please help." This is very simple but very hard to do.

Begin with Yourself

The four mantras work to remove fear, doubt, and isolation. They are not complicated or difficult to understand. And you don't have to say them in Sanskrit or Chinese—English will do just fine. You should learn them by heart, and you must have the courage, the wisdom, and the joy to practice them. The practice of mindfulness, of meditation, consists of coming back to ourselves to restore peace and harmony. The energy that enables us to do this is mindfulness, an energy that also carries with it concentration, understanding, and love. If we come back to ourselves to restore peace and harmony, then it will be much easier to help the other person and restore communication in our relationships.

Caring for yourself, reestablishing peace in yourself, is the basic condition for helping someone else. You can help another person stop bringing suffering on himself and others. Once you know how to defuse the bomb in yourself, you will know how to help your friend defuse the bomb in herself. To be able to help, we need to have at least a little calm, a little joy, a little compassion in us. We get these from practicing mindfulness in everyday life. Mindfulness isn't something we practice only in the meditation hall; we also practice in the kitchen, in the garden, or when we're on the telephone, driving the car, or washing the dishes. Being there with what is beautiful and healing inside us and around us is something we should do each day. And it is possible to do this in all our daily activities.

The Opposite
of Fear

When I met Dr. Martin Luther King Jr. in 1966, during the Vietnam War, one of the things we discussed was the importance of building community—or, as we call it in Buddhism, sangha. Dr. King knew that community building was vital. He was aware that, without a community, little could be accomplished. A solid sense of brotherhood and sisterhood gives us strength when we feel fear or despair and helps sustain our power of love and compassion. Brotherhood and sisterhood can heal and transform our lives. Dr. King spent much of his time building a community that he called "the beloved community."

Our beloved community, our sangha, is a group of people who together practice generating mindfulness, concentration, and insight. Everyone feels embraced and supported by the collective energy generated by the practice. Often, our feelings of loneliness and isolation feed our fears and encourage them to grow. In the sangha, there are people who are solid enough in the practice that they can sit with us and share their energy of mindfulness. We can call on them for support: "Dear brother, dear sister, I need your presence. I have a big pain, and by myself I cannot embrace it. So please help me." We breathe together, and with our combined energy of mindfulness we are able to recognize, embrace, and transform that pain. We know we are part of the sangha river, we are not isolated drops of water, and we will make it to the ocean together.

When there's healing and peace, we know it's a real sangha. With the support of the sangha, the practice is easier, and life in general becomes much easier. Your family or your group of friends can be your sangha. It is whatever community supports you. Building a sangha means building your safety, your support, and your happiness.

Deep Listening and Loving Speech

When communication is cut off, we all suffer. When no one listens to us or understands us, we are like bombs ready to explode. Compassionate listening brings about healing. Sometimes only ten minutes of listening deeply can transform us and bring a smile back to our lips.

Many of us have lost our capacity for listening and using loving speech in our families. It may be that no one is capable of listening to anyone else. So we feel very lonely even within our own families. We go to a therapist, hoping that she will be able to listen to us. But many therapists also have deep suffering within. Sometimes they cannot listen as deeply as they would like. So if we really love someone, we need to train ourselves to be deep listeners.

We also need to train ourselves to use loving speech. We have lost our capacity to say things calmly. We get irritated too easily. Every time we open our mouths, our speech is sour or bitter. We have lost our capacity for speaking with kindness. Without this ability, we cannot succeed in restoring harmony, love, and happiness.

In Buddhism, we speak of bodhisattvas, wise and compassionate beings who stay on Earth to alleviate the suffering of others. The bodhisattva Avalokiteshvara, also called Quan Yin, has a great capacity for listening with compassion and true presence. Quan Yin is the bodhisattva who can listen and understand the sounds of the world, the cries of suffering.

You have to practice breathing mindfully in and out so that compassion always stays with you. You listen without giving advice or passing judgment. You can say to yourself about the other person, "I am listening to him just because I want to relieve his suffering." This is called *compassionate listening*. You have to listen in such a way that compassion remains with you the whole time you are listening. That is the art. If halfway through listening, irritation or anger comes up, then you cannot listen deeply anymore. You have to practice in such a way that every time the energy of irritation and anger comes up, you can breathe in and out mindfully and continue to hold compassion within you. No matter what the other person says, even if there is a lot of injustice in his way of seeing things, even if he condemns or blames you, you continue to sit very quietly, breathing in and out.

If you are not in good shape, if you don't feel that you can go on listening in this way, let the other person know. Ask your friend, "Dear one, can we continue in a few days? I need to renew myself. I need to practice so that I can listen to you in the best way I can." Practice more walking meditation, more mindful breathing, and more sitting meditation to restore your capacity for compassionate listening.

Walking with the Sangha

One wonderful thing to do with your community is walking meditation. When we are physically active together, moving, it is easy to feel supported by the collective energy. It is good to begin your practice of walking meditation with a group to get the support. You can ask a friend to go with you, or you can even take the hand of a child and walk with him or her.

To practice mindful walking on your own, you can begin by making a contract with a staircase: you vow that you will always go up or down that staircase mindfully, with very solid steps. If it happens that halfway up you realize that one of your steps didn't have your true presence in it, you go down and begin again. If you can do it successfully with that staircase, then wherever you go you'll be able to dwell in the present moment. You also can make a contract with a particular distance, perhaps from your work area to the restroom, and vow that when you walk that distance every step will be solid and mindful; otherwise you will go back and do it again. It's a wonderful way to learn how to live every moment of your daily life deeply, resisting being carried away by your habit energy. Walk with your feet, not with your head. Bring your attention to your feet and walk. Walk in such a way that joy and real life are possible right here and now.

When we do walking meditation as a group, we produce a collective energy of mindfulness and peace that nourishes us and helps heal us.

Collective Mindfulness

We can continue improving the quality of our practice by being in regular contact with our community. A community of practitioners generating a collective energy of mindfulness and concentration will help us a lot. Particularly when we're just beginning to practice, our mindfulness and concentration might not be strong enough for us to recognize and embrace our pain, our sorrow, and our fear. With a community supporting us, we have a better chance.

When we are suffering, we can come to the sangha and say, "Dear friends, this is my pain, my despair, my anger; it is too much for me. Please help to hold this block of pain and sorrow and fear in me." We allow the sangha to embrace us, to carry us with its powerful collective energy of mindfulness and concentration; suddenly we feel that we are able to be with our fear and embrace our pain and sorrow. Sitting with the sangha like that, practicing breathing mindfully in and out, will bring you relief and begin to transform and heal you. The presence of a sangha in our life as a practitioner is very important, so as a practitioner, we always think of helping to build a sangha in our neighborhood, where we live.

In the Buddhist tradition, we call our practice our *Dharma body*. We have our physical body, but if we have a spiritual practice, we also have another body, our Dharma body. With the Dharma body, we can cope with difficulties and suffering, and if our Dharma body is strong, we can help other people.

Dharma may be understood as the wise teachings. There is the spoken Dharma and the written Dharma, but there is also a living Dharma. When we practice mindful breathing, when we practice walking meditation, even if we don't say anything and we don't listen to any Dharma talk, we are embodying the living Dharma. When you see a brother or sister who walks mindfully and enjoys every step, you see that she is embodying the living Dharma. Radiating peace and joy and life all around is what we call the *living Dharma*.

The Buddha's Sangha

The first thing the Buddha did after his enlightenment at the foot of the Bodhi tree was to look around for elements with which to build a sangha. The Buddha knew, just as Dr. King understood more than twenty-five centuries later, that without a sangha he could not accomplish his dream, his career as a buddha. Without a community, without a sangha, a buddha cannot do very much. It's like a musician with no instrument. The Buddha was an excellent sangha builder. In no time at all, he built a monastic sangha of 1,250 people. It wasn't always easy, but he learned. We too can learn to build a sangha.

We are all aware that suffering is there in ourselves and in the world. We want to do something, to be something, to help reduce the suffering. Many of us feel helpless because the suffering is so great. On our own, it doesn't seem that we can do much to alleviate that suffering. It's overwhelming. We become sick and depressed. When the Buddha was a young man, he had the same feeling. He saw all the suffering around him. He saw that even as a king, he wouldn't be able to do much to change it. So he decided not to become a king. He sought another way. What motivated him to become a monk, to practice, was his deep desire to help people suffer less.

Monks, nuns, and lay practitioners are motivated by the same desire as the Buddha: to do something to alleviate the suffering in ourselves and in the world. The suffering inside us reflects the suffering in the world. If we understand our suffering, we understand the suffering of the world; if we can transform our own suffering, we'll be able to help transform the suffering in the world. And that's precisely what the Buddha did.

When I was a young monk in Vietnam during the decades of war, the suffering was immense. Millions of people died—not just soldiers, but many civilians; not only adults, but also children. We were inundated with suffering. We wanted to do something to end the war. I saw very clearly that we could do very little if we acted on our own; we had to come together as a sangha, and then we could do a lot.

Everyone feels very much the same. Our planet is beset by so much danger. There's so much violence and suffering in the world. If you allow the plague of helplessness to overwhelm you, you'll go insane. You want to *do* something—first of all to survive, and then to help reduce the suffering. And we've seen, just as the Buddha saw, that if we don't have a sangha, we can't do very much. So we come together and we stick to the sangha through thick and thin, because we know that there is no way out of this situation except with a sangha.

When we see the suffering of the world, we know that by comparison the suffering inside us is hardly anything. That realization lessens our suffering right away. Getting in touch with the suffering of the world, we feel much less alone, and our own suffering feels smaller already. Coming together as a sangha, we have a collective aspiration. There is a collective willingness, energy, and desire. That's the kind of energy that helps us realize how very much we can do together. I believe that the next buddha will no longer be an individual; it will be a sangha, because one buddha is no longer enough. We have to be a sangha.

We can come together in a way that nourishes our joy as well as our sense of shared humanity. We feel joy in doing things together as a sangha, smiling, singing, working together. During the time we're together, we develop our happiness, our purification, and our aspiration. As our aspiration becomes stronger and stronger, we can face many difficulties and take action together to help reduce the suffering in the world.

We can get a lot of joy working together as a sangha. That kind of joy will heal us and help heal the world. Without the joy of brotherhood and sisterhood, we cannot go very far. Loving kindness is nothing but brotherhood and sisterhood, understanding, and a nurturing love. It's not romantic love. Romantic love is not enough. It's short-lived. Brotherhood and sisterhood is a long-lasting love that can sustain us and help us realize our vow.

We should get in touch with the awareness that, without a sangha, without being genuinely together, we cannot help transform the world's fear and suffering. We should learn how to breathe in and out to release our tension and embrace our painful feelings. When there is a feeling of fear, anger, or despair, we have to know how to take care of that feeling. When there is a conflict, we have to know how to practice deep listening, compassionate listening, and loving speech in order to restore communication. That is something we can learn only if we know how to practice. Our practice helps transform the suffering in ourselves, in our families, in our community, and in the world. But the practice will not be easy if there is no sangha.

Building Your Sangha

The first thing we need to do is to look around and identify the elements of our sangha. We have to start like the Buddha did. We mustn't wait for our next retreat or summer vacation; we need to join a sangha or start building a sangha right away at home. Then we can continue our practice. We can do walking, sitting, breathing, listening to the bell in mindfulness. Sangha building is a very important and noble work. Every one of us should think of doing this as soon as possible. Please build a sangha, a true one, a community that can generate brotherhood and sisterhood, peace, and the energy of mindfulness.

If there isn't an existing sangha that is close enough or suitable for you, please start a sangha in your home, in your town, and create a refuge for yourself, your children, your friends, and your family. Group energy is stronger than our individual energy by itself, and if you know how to borrow from it, you will be strong enough to hold your feelings and not be over-whelmed by suffering.

When you throw a rock into the river, no matter how small it is, it will sink to the bottom. But if you have a boat, you can keep many rocks afloat. The same is true of a sangha. If you are alone, you may sink into the river of suffering, but if you have a community of practice to help carry you and you allow it to embrace your pain and sorrow, you will float. Many of us have benefited greatly from the collective energy of the sangha. If you see that the sangha is precious and crucial for your practice, try your best to get a group of people to practice with you, and everyone will benefit. That is your lifeboat.

When you practice well, you become a refuge for yourself and also for your loved ones. If you transform your family into a sangha, other people can come and take refuge in your family. If you're able to bring a few families together, you set up a sangha, and if the practice goes well in your group, it becomes a refuge for many other people. When we're in a sangha, we're like a drop in a great river. We allow the sangha to hold us and transport us, and our fear, pain, and suffering are recognized, embraced, and transformed.

Practices for Transforming Fear

Releasing Fear from Body and Feelings: Eight Simple Mindfulness Exercises

Practicing mindful breathing helps us experience joy and peace. When we concentrate on our breath, we're not carried off by thoughts about the past or the future. We're free of all thinking. When we're lost in thought, we can't be really present. Descartes said, "I think, therefore I am"; but most of the time, the truth is more like "I think, therefore I am not really here."

When we bring our attention to our in-breath, we're not *thinking* about our in-breath; it's direct experience. We're *living* our in-breath. Our in-breath is not a thought; it's a reality. We are living the reality that is our in-breath. "Breathing in, I enjoy my in-breath." When we breathe this way, in mindfulness, we can see many things. We can touch the miracle of life, because when we breathe mindfully, we realize that we're alive. To be alive is a fantastic thing. To be present in the here and now, breathing, is a miracle. To be alive is one of the greatest of miracles. Parents holding their newborn child know this; people on their deathbeds know it too. To be alive, breathing, taking steps on this planet, is a wonderful thing. We don't need to drink some wine or host a dinner party to celebrate life; we can celebrate in every moment with our breathing and our steps. With mindfulness and concentration, we can get in touch and live every moment of our daily lives as a miracle. And we can do it right now, today.

The energy of mindfulness can be generated anytime, anywhere. With mindful breathing, mindful walking, that energy brings us deeply in touch with the wonders of life, and that's what brings us happiness. Our practice is very concrete, very simple. When you breathe in and really pay attention to your in-breath, there will be a change right away. You are more there, and you touch more of reality. When you practice walking meditation, you walk so mindfully that you're able to be in touch with reality in a deeper way. And you begin to live your life more deeply. How closely you're in touch with reality depends on your way of breathing and looking.

Here are some simple exercises of mindful breathing to use whenever fear arises. Exercises 1 through 4 are for taking care of the body; exercises 5 through 8 are for taking care of the feelings.

Exercise One

The first exercise is extremely simple, but it brings great benefit: the insight that you are really here, alive. And you're not only this body, but also your environment—you're all of this. The practice is so simple, yet it can bring the miracles of joy and happiness.

The first exercise is, "Breathing in, I know this is an in-breath. Breathing out, I know this is an out-breath." We recognize the in-breath as an in-breath and the out-breath as an out-breath. It's easy. When we do that, we bring our attention to the in- and out-breath. We let go of our thinking; we let go of the past, of the future, of our projects. We are only with our breath, and we are free. Our in-breath becomes the sole object of our attention and awareness. We can enjoy just breathing.

Exercise Two

The second exercise is, "Breathing in, I follow my in-breath all the way from the beginning to the end. Breathing out, I follow my out-breath all the way from the beginning to the end." The in-breath may last two seconds, five seconds, or more. You follow the entire in-breath from the very beginning to the very end, without any interruption, and you enjoy the whole journey, the whole length of the breath. In that way your concentration becomes stronger and stronger. That's how we train ourselves in concentration. Mindfulness carries within it the energy of concentration, and with concentration, conditions are ripe for insight to manifest at any moment.

So the first exercise is the identification of the in-breath and the out-breath. The second exercise involves staying with the in-breath and the out-breath for their whole length.

Exercise Three

The third exercise is, "Breathing in, I'm aware of my whole body. Breathing out, I'm aware of my whole body." During the length of the in-breath you get in touch with your physical body, and your body becomes the object of your mindfulness. That means bringing the mind back to the body. There's a reunification, a reunion of the body and the mind, so that you are truly present, body and mind together. Oneness of body and mind is the object of the third exercise. "Breathing in, I'm aware of my whole body." This is an act of reconciliation between the mind and the body.

Perhaps you've abandoned and neglected your body for some time. You may not have taken good care of your body in the way you eat or the way you work. So this is a moment when you bring your awareness back to your body and care for and reconcile with your body: "Breathing in, I'm aware of my whole body." And we know very well that, breathing like this, you're really here, you're really alive, and you have something to offer to other people. You're here for yourself, and you're here for others.

Exercise Four

We should apply this practice in our daily lives. Being with your body, you can see what's going on in the body. You may recognize that there's tension or pain in the body. Perhaps the pain is chronic, because you've allowed it to go on like that for a long time. You've allowed the tension and pain to accumulate in the body. Now, as you return to the body, you can do something to release the tension and reduce the pain. That's why the Buddha offered us the fourth exercise: "Breathing in, I am aware of some tension and pain in my body; breathing out, I calm and release the tension and pain in my body."

The third exercise is recognizing the existence of the body, and the fourth exercise is releasing tension, allowing the tension to flow out of the body. "Breathing in, I'm aware of my whole body. Breathing out, I'm aware of my whole body." "Breathing in, I am aware of some tension and pain in my body; breathing out, I calm and release the tension and pain in my body." When tension is released, pain is reduced.

So with the first four exercises, we learn to handle our breathing and our body, to take care of our body. "I am not just my thoughts and projects; I have a body. I want to take good care of my body and handle it well. The breath is part of my body." And since everything is connected, we're already starting to get in touch with feelings, because when we get in touch with our body we recognize the tension, the pain.

Tension produces an unpleasant sensation, an unpleasant feeling. Pain is also an unpleasant feeling. Because of that, we practice letting go. We release the tension so that we can feel better and reduce the pain in the body. These exercises of mindful breathing are very methodical.

The Realm of Feelings

In the next four exercises, we move fully into the realm of feelings. The fifth exercise consists of bringing forth a pleasant feeling, a feeling of joy. When we practice mindfulness, we should be capable of generating a feeling of joy, a feeling of happiness. In Buddhism we often speak of how we can take care of suffering, but we also speak of joy. A practitioner should know how to take care of happiness as well as suffering. The fifth and the sixth exercises are for bringing forth joy and happiness. The seventh exercise is for taking care of pain and suffering. There is a reason these exercises speak about happiness first and suffering after. We need some joy and happiness to give us the strength to transform suffering.

"Breathing in, I recognize a pleasant feeling." Traditionally we say there are three kinds of feelings: pleasant feelings, unpleasant feelings, and neutral feelings. For me there's also a fourth one: a mixed feeling, when happiness and pain are mixed up together, like a bittersweet feeling.

The fifth and sixth exercises are for recognizing feelings that are pleasant. You can recognize a pleasant feeling when it manifests. Or you can bring up a pleasant feeling at any moment. Since you're a practitioner of mindfulness, you know how to recognize a feeling of happiness, and you can also produce a feeling of happiness. With mindfulness and concentration, it's always possible to bring forth a feeling of happiness.

The Conditions of Happiness

There are so many conditions of happiness available in the present moment. You can take a piece of paper and a pencil and write them all down. In the beginning, you may think your list won't be very long. But you'll be surprised to find that even both sides of the paper aren't enough for writing down all the conditions of happiness that are already available.

When we look at our own body and the environment, we can identify many conditions of happiness that are already available—hundreds, thousands of them. For example, your eyes are a condition of happiness. When you have eyes still in good condition, you need only to open them to see a paradise of shapes and colors. When we've lost our eyesight, we recognize that to have good vision is a wonder. So your good eyesight is already a condition of happiness. Thanks to your eyes being in good condition, this whole paradise is available to you. If you touch this condition with awareness, happiness naturally arises.

There are innumerable other wonders just like that in your life. For example, there is your heart. "Breathing in, I'm aware of my heart." With mindfulness you recognize the presence of your heart. "Breathing in, I know my heart is there, and I'm very happy." To have a heart that functions normally is a great happiness. When you've worked a long shift, you may have a chance to take a rest, but your heart never stops working; it's beating for you twenty-four hours a day. Your heart is healthy and working for you; that's a wonderful thing. There are those among us who don't have such a heart, who are always afraid of having a heart attack or some other emergency. There's nothing in the world they want more than to have a normal heart just like the one you have. So you breathe and recognize the presence of your heart, and you are touching another condition of happiness. "Breathing in, I'm aware of my heart. Breathing out, I smile to my heart with a lot of gratitude." You're touching another condition of happiness. You can touch hundreds of conditions of happiness right there in your own body and mind, as well as around you.

With mindfulness and concentration, it's always possible to bring forth a feeling of happiness. All we have to do is to come back to ourselves so we can recognize the conditions of happiness that are available, and then happiness comes right away. Someone who practices mindfulness can always generate a feeling of happiness, anytime, anyplace.

If you're capable of producing a feeling of joy, a feeling of happiness, then you'll also be able to handle painful feelings. A person who doesn't practice doesn't know how to deal with painful feelings or strong emotions. But for those of us who are practitioners, when a painful feeling or a strong emotion comes up, we're not victims—we know what to do. When a feeling of happiness or suffering comes up, we just recognize the feeling as it is. Even with a pleasant feeling, we just recognize it. We don't need to grasp it or cling to it. We just practice mere recognition of what is happening, that is, a pleasant feeling.

We don't try to grab on to the pleasant sensation, and we don't try to push it away. We just acknowledge its existence. When a painful feeling comes, we do the same thing. We don't need to grab onto, fight, or repress the unpleasant feeling. We simply recognize its presence. We stay free, even when we have a painful feeling. A feeling is just a feeling. And you are much more than that feeling. We shouldn't let ourselves be carried away by a feeling, even a pleasant one, much less an unpleasant one. We just practice recognition of the feeling.

Recognizing Joy and Happiness

The fifth exercise is to recognize a feeling of joy: "Breathing in, I feel joy. Breathing out, I know joy is there." And the sixth is to recognize a feeling of happiness: "Breathing in, I feel happy. Breathing out, I know happiness is there." Buddhist teachings draw a slight distinction between joy and happiness. Imagine someone is walking in a desert, is very thirsty, and has nothing to drink. All of a sudden he sees an oasis ahead, and he knows he's going to be able to drink there. "In about fifteen minutes I'll be there and I'll have water to drink!" That's the feeling of joy. When our friend arrives at the oasis, kneels down, and drinks the water, then there is the sensation of happiness. Joy and happiness are slightly different. In the joy there's still a little bit of excitement. Happiness is a more peaceful feeling, like contentment.

We have to be there for our feelings. There's a whole river of feelings flowing in us day and night. Every feeling is a drop in that river. A feeling is born, manifests, stays for a time, and then passes away. We can sit on the bank of the river of feelings and observe, recognizing each feeling as it manifests, seeing it remain, and seeing it pass away. We shouldn't identify ourselves with the feeling, nor should we try to push it away. We're free, even from our own feelings. We have to train ourselves to recognize feelings. And with mindfulness we can bring forth a feeling of well-being, a feeling of happiness, at any time.

Recognizing and Embracing Pain

The seventh exercise is to recognize a painful or unpleasant feeling: "Breathing in, I know that a painful feeling is there. Breathing out, I calm that painful feeling." Pain is a kind of energy, and a nonpractitioner can be overtaken by that painful feeling. We become a victim of the painful feeling, whether it's a sensation in the body or an emotion. There are strong emotions that are very painful, zones of energy that manifest from the depths of our consciousness.

Every time a painful feeling or emotion comes up, the practitioner should know how to handle that feeling. The method the Buddha proposed is to get in touch with the seed of mindfulness in us. We can breathe, we can walk, to generate mindfulness as a second zone of energy that will be able to take care of the first energy, the painful feeling. It's so important for us to train ourselves in breathing mindfully and walking mindfully so we will know how to generate the energy of mindfulness and concentration. It's precisely with that energy that we'll be able to handle the painful feeling. The second zone of energy, which is mindfulness and concentration, comes up and embraces the first zone of energy, the painful feeling. We follow this method exactly. With the energy of mindfulness and concentration, we just recognize and embrace the painful feeling. "Hello, my fear. Hello, my anger. Hello, my sadness. I know you are there. I'm going to take good care of you."

There's the energy of the pain, and there's also the energy of mindfulness and concentration. When that positive energy embraces the painful energy, there will be an effect. The energy of mindfulness will penetrate, like heat waves or sunlight. In the earliest hours of the morning, a lotus flower is still closed. As the sun comes up, the sunlight begins to touch the petals. The sunlight doesn't just surround the lotus flower; its photons actually penetrate the lotus flower with energy, and soon the flower will open. That is exactly the same as what we do. When we embrace our pain, particles of the energy of mindfulness and concentration begin to penetrate, like photons, into the zone of pain. And this will bring relief after some minutes. It's like when a room is cold, you turn on your radiator, and it emits waves of heat. Those heat waves don't chase out the cold; they embrace and permeate the cold air, and after some time, the air becomes warmer. There's no violence in this; there's no fighting. That's what a practitioner does. Mindfulness and concentration embrace the pain.

Relief from Fear

The eighth exercise is to calm and release the tension in the painful feeling—to embrace, soothe, and bring relief to the feeling: "Breathing in, I calm my mental formations. Breathing out, I calm my mental formations." This exercise is exactly like what we did with the body. First we recognized the presence of the body, and then we brought some relief. Here we do the same with the feelings. We recognize the pain, and we bring relief.

We embrace our feelings with tenderness, with nonviolence, and we soothe those feelings. A few minutes may be enough to bring relief. As a practitioner we must be capable of recognizing, embracing, and relieving our suffering. If you're a beginner and your energy of mindfulness is not yet solid enough to be able to recognize and embrace suffering, please ask a friend to help.

After some minutes of being recognized and embraced, that painful feeling's zone of energy will recede, and you will feel a welcome relief from the grip of fear or pain. A seed from the depths of consciousness manifests, it stays for a while as a zone of energy, and then it goes back down to its original place as a seed. But after being recognized and embraced with mindfulness, it loses some of its strength. The seed is a bit weaker than before it manifested. You know how to do this; you know very well how to take care of your pain. Every time the pain manifests, we have to let it manifest; we should not push it down. We shouldn't try to suppress it. We have to let it come and take good care of it.

When we practice walking meditation, when we breathe mindfully, we generate the powerful energy of mindfulness, which can recognize and embrace our suffering and fear. After doing that for a time, you will see that the fear goes back down to its former place as a seed, and you'll understand that the next time it manifests, you'll be able to do exactly the same thing. Your chronic fear and anxiety will be genuinely reduced.

The more we practice, the more we are gentle with our fear and are able to embrace it, the more the fear goes away. It is possible to live a life in the present moment completely without fear. Without fear, we are able to see more clearly our connections to others. Without fear, we have more room for understanding and compassion. Without fear, we are truly free.

Transforming the Roots of Fear in the Mind: Eight Breathing Exercises

These eight exercises continue the first eight exercises. They can help us understand our mind and let go of illusions, so that we can touch the true nature of reality and attain fearlessness.

The Realm of the Mind

The first exercise is to be aware of our minds and recognize the state of our minds, just as the third exercise is awareness of the body and the seventh is awareness of the feelings. "Breathing in, I am aware of my mind. Breathing out, I am aware of my mind."

There's a river of mind in which every thought is a drop of water. We sit on the bank of the river and observe the manifestation and fading of each thought. We can simply recognize them as they arise, as they stay for some time, as they go away. We don't need to grasp or fight or push them away.

When fear is there, we say: "Breathing in, I know the mental formation of fear is in me."

When the mental formation of fear is there, we breathe in and recognize the presence of fear in us. With mindfulness and concentration, we recognize and embrace the mental formation that is there. Then we can look deeply into the nature of that mental formation.

Making the Mind Happy and at Ease

The second exercise is gladdening the mind: "Breathing in, I make my mind happy. Breathing out, I make my mind happy."

We make the mind glad so as to strengthen it and give it vitality. This is like the practice of generating joy and happiness in the previous set of exercises, with an added element of re-invigorating and energizing the mind.

According to Buddhist psychology, the mind has at least two layers. The lower layer is called store consciousness, and all the seeds of the mental formations are there. When a seed is touched or watered, it manifests in mind consciousness as a mental formation. To gladden the mind, we use a practice called *selective watering*.

First, we allow the negative seeds to sleep in our store consciousness and don't give them a chance to manifest; if they manifest too often, their base will be strengthened. Second, if a negative seed manifests in mind consciousness, we help it go back to store consciousness as quickly as possible, where it can sleep as a seed. The third practice is to encourage wholesome mental formations to manifest in our conscious mind. In the fourth practice, when a good mental formation has manifested, we try to keep it there as long as we can. We should organize our life so that the seeds of our wholesome mental formations can be touched and watered several times a day. There are good seeds in store consciousness that may not have been able to manifest previously, and now we give them a chance.

Concentrating the Mind

The third exercise is to bring the mind into concentration. We practice concentration to get insight: "Breathing in, I concentrate my mind. Breathing out, I concentrate my mind."

Concentration has the power to burn away afflictions, just like sunlight focused by a lens can burn a piece of paper underneath. In the same way, concentration—looking deeply into our fear, anger, delusion, and despair—can burn them away, leaving insight.

One concentration is the concentration on emptiness, the absence of a permanent entity. Although emptiness isn't difficult to understand and it's real, still we're not used to thinking in that way. So we have to train ourselves to look in such a way as to see things more deeply and see their ultimately empty nature.

Scientists tell us that all objects are made mainly of space and that the amount of matter in a flower or a table is almost nothing at all—put together, all the matter in a table would be smaller than a grain of salt. We know that's the truth, but in our daily lives we still think of the table as something big and solid. When scientists enter the world of elementary particles, they have to put aside their habitual way of looking at things as existing separately from each other. Then they have a chance of understanding what's really going on in the world of matter. Even scientists have to train themselves. So you have to train yourself to see like that in your daily life.

Concentration means you keep the insight alive for a long time. It's not just a flash; that's not enough to liberate you. So in your daily life, you keep that insight of nonself, of emptiness, of impermanence alive. When you see a person, a bird, a tree, or a rock, you see its nature of emptiness. Then it becomes an insight that will liberate you. It's very different from speculating about the meaning of emptiness. You have to really *see* the nature of emptiness in yourself and others. Once that insight is there, you're no longer afraid, no longer bound, no longer a victim of separation and discrimination, because you've seen the nature of interbeing. Meditating deeply, looking deeply into the nature of whatever is there, you can touch the nature of interbeing in it. Whether it is a flower, a buddha, a person, or a tree, you touch the nature of emptiness and interbeing, and you see that the one contains the all.

Liberating the Mind

With the fourth exercise, we free our minds from afflictions and notions: "Breathing in, I liberate my mind. Breathing out, I liberate my mind."

Our minds are tied up, bound by afflictions such as fear, anger, sorrow, and discrimination. We have practiced being aware of and embracing our fear and our pain, but to fully transform them we need the strength of our concentration to liberate ourselves from these binding forces.

There are many types of concentration we can practice. One is the concentration on impermanence. We have a notion of impermanence. Even though we accept and agree that things are impermanent, our notion of impermanence remains and determines how we see things and how we behave in our daily life. Although we know intellectually that our beloved is impermanent, we still live and behave as though our loved ones will always be there and we will always be the same people we are now. But everything is changing in every moment, like a river. When we see him again, we may be in touch with the person of twenty years ago; we cannot touch the person of the present moment, who has a different way of thinking and feeling. So we meditate on impermanence in order to touch the nature of impermanence. We need the concentration on impermanence, not the notion of impermanence. The notion of impermanence cannot liberate us. It's the insight of impermanence that liberates us. It's something altogether different from the notion.

But in the beginning, we can use the teaching, the notion of impermanence, as an instrument to help bring about the insight of impermanence. It's like a match and a flame. The match is not the flame, but the match can bring about the flame. And when we have the flame, the flame will consume the match. When we have the insight, the insight will burn away the notion. What we need for our liberation is the insight of impermanence.

Perception

With these final four exercises, we investigate the nature of the objects of our mind—that is, how we perceive things. These concentrations help us get a correct perception of reality, of the world. Many of us are still caught in the notion that consciousness is inside us and the objective world is out there. We believe that our consciousness is here, and we're trying to reach out and understand the objective world out there. When we look at things in terms of interbeing, we see that the subject and object of consciousness cannot exist separately. It's like left and right; one can't exist without the other.

Whenever we perceive something, whether it's a pen or a flower, the object of perception and the subject of perception always manifest at the same time. When we are conscious, we are always conscious of something; when we are mindful, we are always mindful of something; when we think, we always think about something. So object and subject manifest at the same time.

Contemplating Impermanence

The fifth exercise is the concentration on impermanence, the practice of which I have already described in detail as an example illustrating the preceding exercise, liberating the mind. "Breathing in, I observe the impermanent nature of all Dharmas. Breathing out, I observe the impermanent nature of all Dharmas."

Impermanence is just one type of concentration. But if we do it well, we also succeed in other concentrations at the same time. Going deeply into impermanence, we discover no-self, emptiness, and interbeing. So impermanence represents all concentrations. While breathing in and breathing out, we keep our concentration on impermanence alive until we can make a breakthrough into the heart of reality. The object of our observation may be a flower, a pebble, someone we love, or someone we hate; it may be us, our pain, our fear, or our sorrow. Anything can serve as the object of our meditation. Our intention is to touch the nature of impermanence in it.

Letting Go of Craving

The sixth exercise involves contemplating nondesire, noncraving: "Breathing in, I observe the disappearance of desire. Breathing out, I observe the disappearance of desire."

There is another consciousness that is between store consciousness and the upper layer of the mind, called *manas*. Manas is born from store and serves as the base of mind consciousness. Manas contains a lot of delusion and therefore has the tendency to grasp; it is the part of our mind that is always seeking pleasure and ignoring the dangers of pleasure seeking. It is manas that carries our original fear and desire. The contemplation of impermanence can help us transform the delusion in manas so it becomes wisdom. We look deeply into the object of our craving to see its true nature. The object of our craving may be something or someone who has the capacity to destroy our body and our mind. Looking deeply into what we desire and what we consume is a critical practice. What we bring into our body and mind every day may be feeding our grasping, fear, and violence.

Nirvana

"Breathing in, I observe cessation. Breathing out, I observe cessation."

In the seventh exercise we observe cessation—nirvana, the extinction of all notions—so that we can touch reality as it truly is. Then we touch our interbeing nature and know we are part of the whole cosmos. The nature of reality transcends all notions and ideas, including the notions of birth and death, being and nonbeing, coming and going. Contemplating impermanence, no-self, emptiness, no-birth, and no-death can lead to liberation. The notions of birth and death can be a source of fear, anguish, and anxiety. Seeing the no-birth, no-death nature of reality, we free ourselves of anxiety and fear.

Letting Go

"Breathing in, I observe letting go. Breathing out, I observe letting go."

This exercise helps us look deeply at giving up craving, hatred, and fear. This concentration helps us touch the true nature of reality and brings the wisdom that can liberate us from fear, anger, and despair. We let go of our wrong perceptions of reality so as to be free. *Nirvana* literally means cooling, the putting out of flames; in Buddhism, it refers to extinction of the afflictions brought about by our wrong perceptions. Nirvana isn't a place to go or something belonging to the future. Nirvana is the true nature of reality, things as they are. Nirvana is available in the here and now. You are already in nirvana; you *are* nirvana, just as the wave is already the water.

Our true nature is no-beginning, no-end; no-birth, no-death. If we know how to touch our true nature, there's no more fear, no anger, no despair. Our true nature is nirvana. So if someone close to you has just passed away, be sure to look for her in her new manifestation. It's impossible for her to die. She is continued in many ways. Using the eyes of wisdom, you can recognize her around you and inside you. And you can continue to talk to her: "Darling, I know you are still there in your new form. It's impossible for you to die." The eighth exercise helps us release our illusions and be in touch with the true nature of reality. This gives us freedom and relief and brings us a lot of happiness.

We need to continue learning, practicing, and discussing, so our understanding continues to grow. Dwelling in the present moment, you'll find that you become very interested in investigating all of life, and you can discover many wonderful things, many wonderful ways to practice. This doesn't mean you get lost in your thinking; it means you observe reality as it is and discover its true nature.

We live in fear of many things—of our past, of death, of losing our "self" or identity. These eight exercises, together with the first eight breathing exercises, bring us the insight that enables us to touch the ultimate dimension of reality and free ourselves from fear. When we are able to share our way of being and our insight with others, we offer them the greatest gift there is, the gift of nonfear.

Deep Relaxation for Transforming Fear and Stress

Fear can accumulate in our body, causing stress and tension. Rest is a precondition for healing. When animals in the forest get wounded, they find a place to lie down, and they rest completely for many days. They don't think about food or anything else. They just rest, and they are able to heal themselves quite naturally. When we humans become fearful and overwhelmed with stress, we may go to the pharmacy and get drugs, but we rarely have the wisdom to stop our running around. We don't know how to help ourselves.

Deep relaxation is an opportunity for our body to rest, heal, and restore itself. We relax our body, give our attention to each part in turn, and send our love and care to every cell. Deep relaxation of the body should be done at least once a day. It may last for twenty minutes or longer. You can do it in bed at night or in the morning. You can also do it whenever it's convenient, in the living room or anywhere you have space where you can lie down and not be disturbed. It's also possible to practice deep relaxation in a sitting position, for example at your office desk.

If your fear and anxiety keep you up at night, deep relaxation can help. Lying awake, you can enjoy the practice of total relaxation and follow your breathing in and out. Sometimes it can help you get some sleep. But even if you don't sleep, it will still nourish you and allow you to rest. It's very important to allow yourself to rest, and this relaxation practice can even be more deeply restful than sleep if our sleep tends to be filled with nightmares or other intense dreams.

When we do deep relaxation in a group, one person guides the exercise using the following cues or some variation of them. When you do deep relaxation on your own, you may like to try doing it as you read, or listen to a recording.

Deep Relaxation Exercise

Lie down on your back with your arms at your sides. Make yourself comfortable. Allow your body to relax. Be aware of the floor beneath you . . . and of the contact of your body with the floor. (*The reader may pause here to breathe.*) Allow your body to sink into the floor. (*Breathe.*)

Become aware of your breathing, in and out. Be aware of your abdomen rising and falling as you breathe in and out. (*Breathe.*) Rising . . . falling . . . rising . . . falling. (*Breathe.*)

Breathing in, bring your awareness to your eyes. Breathing out, allow your eyes to relax. Allow your eyes to sink back into your head. . . . Let go of the tension in all the tiny muscles around your eyes. . . . Our eyes allow us to see a paradise of shapes and colors. . . . Allow your eyes now to rest. . . . Send love and gratitude to your eyes. . . . (*Breathe.*)

You may say to yourself, "Breathing in, I am aware of my eyes. Breathing out, I smile to my eyes."

Breathing in, bring your awareness to your mouth. Breathing out, allow your mouth to relax. Release the tension around your mouth. . . . Your lips are the petals of a flower. . . . Let a gentle smile bloom on your lips. . . . Smiling releases the tension in the dozens of muscles in your face. . . . Feel the tension release in your cheeks . . . your jaw . . . your throat . . . (*Breathe.*)

Breathing in, bring your awareness to your shoulders. Breathing out, allow your shoulders to relax. Let them sink into the floor. . . . Let all the accumulated tension flow into the floor. . . . You carry so much on your shoulders. . . . Now let them relax, as you care for your shoulders. (*Breathe.*)

Breathing in, become aware of your arms. Breathing out, relax your arms. Let your arms sink into the floor . . . your upper arms . . . your elbows . . . your lower arms . . . your wrists . . . hands . . . fingers . . . all the tiny muscles. . . . Move your fingers a little if you need to, to help the muscles relax. (*Breathe.*)

Breathing in, bring your awareness to your heart. Breathing out, allow your heart to relax. (*Breathe.*) . . . You may have neglected your heart for a long time in the way you work, eat, and manage anxiety and stress. (*Breathe.*) . . . Your heart beats for you night and day. Embrace your heart with mindfulness and tenderness, reconciling and taking care of your heart. (*Breathe.*)

Say to yourself as you breathe, "Breathing in, I am aware of my heart. Breathing out, I smile to my heart."

Breathing in, bring your awareness to your legs. Breathing out, allow your legs to relax. Release all the tension in your legs . . . your thighs . . . your knees . . . your calves . . . your ankles . . . your feet . . . your toes . . . all the tiny muscles in your toes. . . . You may want to move your toes a little to help them relax. . . . Send your love and care to your toes. *(Breathe.)*

Breathing in, breathing out. . . . Your whole body feels light . . . like duckweed floating on the water. . . . You have nowhere to go . . . nothing to do. . . . You are as free as the cloud floating in the sky. . . . *(Breathe.)*

Bring your awareness back to your breathing. . .to your abdomen rising and falling. *(Breathe.)*

Following your breathing, become aware of your arms and legs. . . . You may want to move them a little and stretch. *(Breathe.)*

If you are doing the practice before sleep, just continue to follow your breathing, breathing in and breathing out.

If you are doing the practice as a break during the day, when you feel ready, slowly sit up. *(Breathe.)*

When you are ready, slowly stand up.

Take a moment and be aware of your breath as you stand there before continuing on to your next activity.

Metta Meditation:
May We Be Free from Fear

When we are in the grips of fear, we close down and can't be compassionate or generous. To love others, we first have to be loving and gentle with ourselves. This meditation helps us first to accept ourselves, including our suffering and happiness at the same time, and then to be able to wish others well.

Metta means loving kindness. We begin this with an aspiration, such as: "May I be free from fear." We look deeply, with all our being, to understand ourselves. Then we can begin to wish others well: "May he/she be free from fear. May they be free from fear." We don't just repeat the words, or imitate others, or strive after some ideal. We don't just say like a parrot, "I love myself. I love all beings." We have to put our heart into it!

When we practice, we observe how much peace, happiness, and lightness we already have. We notice whether we are anxious about accidents or misfortunes, and how much fear or worry is already in us. As we become aware of the feelings inside, our self-understanding deepens. We see how our fears contribute to our unhappiness, and we see the value of loving ourselves and cultivating a heart of compassion.

Metta Practice

This meditation is adapted from the Visuddhimagga (The Path of Purification) by Buddhaghosa, a fifth-century C.E. systematization of the Buddha's teachings.

Sit still, calm your body and breathing, and recite the aspiration to yourself:

May I be peaceful, happy, and light in body and spirit.

May I be safe and free from injury.

May I be free from fear, anxiety, anger, and afflictions.

The sitting position is a wonderful position for practicing this. Sitting still, you are not too preoccupied with other matters, so you can look deeply at yourself as you are, cultivate your love for yourself, and determine the best ways to express this love in the world.

After practicing this way, you can begin to offer this aspiration to others:

May she be peaceful, happy, and light in body and spirit.

May he be peaceful, happy, and light in body and spirit.

May they be peaceful, happy, and light in body and spirit.

May she be safe and free from injury.

May he be safe and free from injury.

May they be safe and free from injury.

May she be free from anger, afflictions, fear, and anxiety.

May he be free from anger, afflictions, fear, and anxiety.

May they be free from anger, afflictions, fear, and anxiety.

When offering this aspiration, try it first on someone you like, then on someone neutral to you, then on someone you love, and finally on someone the mere thought of whom makes you suffer.

To make this practice concrete, you have to be fully able to visualize yourself and the person you are wishing well. According to the Buddha, a human being is made of five elements, called *skandhas* in Sanskrit. These skandhas are form, feelings, perceptions, mental formations, and consciousness. In a way, you are the surveyor, and these elements are your territory.

Begin Metta practice by looking deeply into your body. Ask some questions: How is my body in this moment? How was it in the past? How will it be in the future? Later, when you meditate on someone you like, someone neutral to you, someone you love, and someone you hate, you also begin by looking at the person's physical aspects. Breathing in and out, visualize his face; his way of walking, sitting, and talking; his heart, lungs, kidneys, and all the organs in his body, taking as much time as you need to bring these details into awareness. But always start with yourself. When you see your own five skandhas clearly, understanding and love arise naturally, and you know what to do and what not to do.

Observe your feelings—whether they are pleasant, unpleasant, or neutral. Feelings flow in us like a river, and each feeling is a drop of water in that river. Look into the river of your feelings and see how each feeling came to be. See what has been preventing you from being happy, and do your best to transform those things. Practice touching the wondrous, refreshing, and healing elements that are already in you and in the world. Doing so, you become stronger and better able to love yourself and others.

The Buddha observed, "The person who suffers most in this world is the person who has many wrong perceptions, and most of our perceptions are erroneous." You see a snake in the dark and you panic, but when your friend shines a light on it, you see that it is only a rope. You have to know which wrong perceptions cause suffering. Love meditation helps you learn to look with clarity and serenity so as to improve the way you perceive.

Next, observe your mental formations, the ideas and tendencies within you that lead you to speak and act as you do. Notice how you are influenced by your individual consciousness and also by the collective consciousness of your family, ancestors, and society.

Finally, look at your consciousness. According to Buddhism, consciousness is like a field with every possible kind of seed in it: seeds of love, compassion, joy, and equanimity; seeds of anger, fear, and anxiety; and seeds of mindfulness. Consciousness is the storehouse that contains all these seeds, all the possibilities of what might arise in your mind. Metta meditation can bring the seeds of peace, joy, and love up into your conscious mind as zones of energy, and transform the seeds of fear.

The Five Mindfulness
Trainings

The five mindfulness trainings provide a concrete application of mindfulness in everyday life. Practicing the five mindfulness trainings helps cultivate Right View, which eliminates discrimination, intolerance, anger, fear, and despair. If we live according to the five mindfulness trainings, we are already on the path of a bodhisattva. Knowing we are on that path, we are not lost in fears regarding the future or confusion about our life in the present.

I. Reverence for Life

Aware of the suffering caused by the destruction of life, I am committed to cultivating the insight of interbeing and compassion, as well as learning to protect the lives of people and animals, and to preserve plant and mineral resources. I am determined not to kill, not to let others kill, and not to support any act of killing in the world, in my thinking, or in my way of life. Seeing that harmful actions arise from anger, fear, greed, and intolerance, which in turn come from dualistic and discriminative thinking, I will cultivate openness, nondiscrimination, and nonattachment to views in order to transform violence, fanaticism, and dogmatism in myself and in the world.

2. True Happiness

Aware of the suffering caused by exploitation, social injustice, theft, and oppression, I am committed to practicing generosity in my thoughts, speech, and acts. I am determined not to steal and not to possess anything that should belong to others; I will share my time, energy, and material resources with those who are in need. I will practice looking deeply to see that the happiness and suffering of others are not separate from my own; that true happiness is not possible without understanding and compassion; and that running after wealth, fame, power, and sensual pleasures can bring much suffering and despair. I am aware that happiness depends on my mental attitude and not on external conditions, and that I can live happily in the present moment simply by remembering that I already have more than enough to be happy. I am committed to establishing a livelihood that will help reduce the suffering of living beings on Earth and reverse the progress of global warming.

3. True Love

Aware of the suffering caused by sexual misconduct, I am committed to cultivating responsibility and learning ways to protect the safety and integrity of individuals, couples, families, and society. Knowing that sexual desire is not love and that sexual activity motivated by craving always harms myself as well as others, I am determined not to engage in sexual relations without true love and a deep, long-term commitment established in the presence of family and friends. I will do everything in my power to protect children from sexual abuse and to prevent couples and families from being harmed by sexual misconduct. Seeing that body and mind are one, I am committed to learning appropriate ways to take care of my sexual energy and to cultivate kindness, compassion, joy, patience, inclusiveness, and all elements of true love for my greater happiness and the greater happiness of others. Practicing true love, we know that we will continue beautifully into the future.

4. Loving Speech and Deep Listening

Aware of the suffering caused by unmindful speech and failure to listen, I am committed to cultivating loving speech and compassionate listening to relieve suffering and promote reconciliation and peace in myself and among other people, ethnic and religious groups, and nations. Knowing that words can create happiness or suffering, I am committed to speaking truthfully using words that inspire confidence, joy, and hope. I am determined not to speak when anger manifests in me. I will practice mindful breathing and walking to recognize and look deeply into my anger. I know that the roots of anger can be found in my wrong perceptions and lack of understanding of the suffering in myself and the other person. I will speak and listen in such a way as to help myself and the other person to transform suffering and see the way out of difficult situations.

I am determined not to spread news that I do not know to be certain and not to utter words that can cause division or discord. I will practice diligently with joy and skillfulness so as to nourish my capacity for understanding, love, and inclusiveness, gradually transforming the anger, violence, and fear that lie deep in my consciousness.

5. Nourishment and Healing

Aware of the suffering caused by unmindful consumption, I am committed to cultivating good health, both physical and mental, for myself, my family, and my society by practicing mindful eating, drinking, and consuming. I will practice looking deeply into how I consume. I will be aware of what I eat, what I consume through my senses, and what intentions and mental states I cultivate in my consciousness. I am determined not to gamble or to indulge in alcohol, drugs, or any other products that contain toxins, including harmful websites, electronic games, TV programs, films, magazines, books, and conversations. I will practice coming back to the present moment to be in touch with the refreshing, healing, and nourishing elements in me and around me, neither letting regrets and sorrow drag me back into the past nor letting anxieties, fear, or craving distract me from the present moment. I am determined not to try to cover up loneliness, anxiety, or other suffering by losing myself in consumption. I will contemplate interbeing and consume in a way that preserves peace, joy, and well-being in my body and consciousness, and in the collective body and consciousness of my family, my society, and the earth.

The Five Awarenesses

The five awarenesses allow you to practice mindfulness with someone you love. Reciting these awarenesses together can help strengthen your support for each other in difficult times. They can be a wonderful part of a wedding ceremony, but they can also be used in any relationship where you want to support each other in the practice. The five awarenesses can help any loving relationship become stronger and longer lasting.

1. We are aware that all generations of our ancestors and all future generations are present in us.

2. We are aware of the expectations that our ancestors, our children, and their children have of us.

3. We are aware that our joy, peace, freedom, and harmony are the joy, peace, freedom, and harmony of our ancestors, our children, and their children.

4. We are aware that understanding is the foundation of love.

5. We are aware that blaming and arguing never help us and only create a wider gap between us. Only understanding, trust, and love can help us change and grow.

In the first awareness, we see ourselves as one element in the continuation of our ancestors and as the link to future generations. When we see in this way, we know that by taking good care of our body and consciousness in the present moment, we are taking care of all generations past and future.

The second awareness reminds us that our ancestors have expectations of us and that our children and their children do too. Our happiness is their happiness; our suffering is their suffering. If we look deeply, we will know what our children and grandchildren expect of us.

The third awareness tells us that joy, peace, freedom, and harmony are not individual matters. We have to live in ways that allow our ancestors within to be liberated so as to liberate ourselves. If we do not liberate them, we ourselves will be bound all our lives, and we will transmit that to our children and grandchildren. Now is the time to liberate our parents and ancestors within. We can offer them joy, peace, freedom, and harmony at the same time as we offer joy, peace, freedom, and harmony to ourselves, our children, and their children. This reflects the teaching of interbeing. As long as our ancestors within are still suffering, we cannot really be happy. If we take one step mindfully, freely and happily touching the earth, we do it for all our ancestors and all future generations.

The fourth awareness tells us that where there is understanding, there is love. When we understand someone's suffering, we're motivated to help, and the energies of love and compassion are released. Whatever we do in this spirit will be for the happiness and liberation of the person we love. We have to practice in such a way that whatever we do for others will make them happy. The willingness to love is not enough. When people do not understand each other, it is impossible for them to love each other.

Remember to practice in the context of a community. Do whatever you can to bring happiness to the air, the water, the rocks, the trees, the birds, and the humans. Live your daily life in such a way as to feel the presence of the community with you all the time, and you will receive the kind of energy you need each time you confront difficulties in your life and the life of the world. The world needs you to be mindful, to be aware of what is going on.

We have to live deeply each moment that is given us to live. If you are capable of living deeply one moment of your life, you can learn to live the same way all the other moments of your life. The French poet René Char said, "If you can dwell in one moment, you will discover eternity." Make each moment an occasion to live deeply, happily, in peace. Each moment is a chance for us to make peace with the world, to make peace possible for the world, to make happiness possible for the world. The world needs our happiness. The practice of mindful living can be described as the practice of happiness, the practice of love. We must cultivate in our lives the capacity to be happy, the capacity to be loving. Understanding is the foundation of love. And looking deeply is the basic practice.

We practice the fifth awareness because even though we know that blaming and arguing never help, we forget. Conscious breathing helps us develop the ability to stop at that crucial moment, to keep ourselves from blaming and arguing.

All of us need to change for the better. It is our responsibility to take care of each other. We are the gardeners, the ones who help the flowers grow. If we understand, the flowers will grow beautifully. Goodwill is not enough; we need to learn the art of making others happy. Art is the essence of life, and the substance of art is mindfulness.